She Talks with Angels
A Psychic Medium's
Guide into the Spirit World

D0963842

She Talks with Angels

A Psychic Medium's
Guide into the Spirit World

Michelle Whitedove

WHITEDOVE PRESS

In most instances the names have been changed to protect individuals privacy

WHITEDOVE PRESS
PO Box 550966
Fort Lauderdale, FL 33355
www.michellewhitedove.com

Book design by ColorCraft.

Photography by Maliena Slaymaker

Printed on acid free paper
Printed in the United States of America

Library of congress number 00-091339

ISBN# 0-615-11118-1 $13.95 Soft cover

ISBN# 0-615-11600-0 $22.95 Hard bound

Second Edition

10 9 8 7 6 5 4 3

A Quote to Think About

"Our deepest fear is not that we are inadequate. Our deepest fear is that we are powerful beyond measure. It is our light, not our darkness, that most frightens us. We ask ourselves, "Who am I to be brilliant, gorgeous, talented, fabulous? "

Actually, who are you not to be? You are a child Of God. Your playing small does not serve the world. There is nothing enlightened about shrinking so that other people won't feel insecure around you. We were born to make manifest the glory of God that is within us. It is not just in some of us; it is in everyone. And as we let our own light shine, we unconsciously give permission to other people to do the same.

As we are liberated from our own fear, our presence automatically liberates others."

-Nelson Mandela

*I would like to dedicate this book to
The Great Spirit, my Angels, and Guides
who made this knowledge possible.
They continue to encourage me when
I need it the most.*

*To Shanté and Jason,
Thank you for all of your love and support.
I couldn't have done it without you.*

CONTENTS

MICHELLE, MY FRIEND AND SPIRITUAL TEACHER

I first met Michelle when I moved to Fort Lauderdale in Florida following the death of my husband. I was impressed with her from first sight, her radiant smile combined with long, flowing, blonde hair and amazing blue eyes, giving Michelle the appearance of an earthbound angel.

Though we were strangers at that time, she took my hand and immediately started telling me, quietly and intently, about my husband's death - omitting none of the grisly details. She described in detail how my husband had died. Originally, I had believed he had died as a result of a boating accident. So, I was shocked when Michelle calmly told me, he'd been murdered.

I was amazed by the details she provided, details that only someone who had been with my husband that day could have known. Michelle had certainly never met my husband or me.

Her intensity and confidence were astonishing, despite her relating such a terrible account, I instinctively felt she had told me the exact truth about how my husband died. A sense of release washed over me; as finally, I was able to mentally lay my husband to rest. I was very thankful for Michelle's help in clearing all the questions in my mind.

Soon after my first meeting with Michelle, my father died suddenly. Michelle helped me ease the pain of the sudden loss, she told me that my father often visits with me, he showed himself to her, young and healthy, dressed in white tails and a top hat just like Fred Astaire. Michelle laughed at the sight of him, she said he was now very happy and that I shouldn't be sad. As an avid hunter and fisherman, she couldn't have known my father loved ballroom dancing. Michelle's insightful counseling helped me overcome the tragic loss and pain of losing a father whom I loved very much.

Since then, Michelle has become my best friend, confidant and mentor. She is a very special person, with exceptional medium and psychic skills. I've watched her countless times, as she uses her unique talents to help people achieve their own inner tranquility.

Michelle has taught many people to acknowledge and make contact with their own Guardian Angels. She radiates warmth and serenity, states she has achieved by her constant connection with Spirit guides and her Guardian Angels. Michelle is a teacher who delights in showing people how to open their hearts to love through the powers of prayer and meditation.

Her medium skills are always used to benefit others and she insists that we are all capable of connecting to our own Guardian Angels to help us on the pathways of this life. Counseling and teaching are the main tools she employs to convey her message to those in need of spiritual guidance and she does that by way of public lectures, classroom teaching and private counseling sessions, Michelle has recently brought her message of love and hope to local television networks. She now hosts her own weekly spiritual TV talk show.

Michelle believes interactive forums provide the best setting for demonstrating her abilities, many people visit her lectures looking for help or resolution of their problems, both spiritual and physical. Michelle welcomes their presence and encourages them to ask questions before relaying personal messages to them from the Spirit World.

Michelle has her own incisive views on life, Spirits, Angels and the way that we live our lives. Her views are always presented in her own inimitable down to earth and direct style. Michelle is a different type of psychic - she is warm and always truthful. She goes right to the heart of an issue without resorting to half truths or innuendoes, relaying information exactly the way that 'Spirit' gives it to her, without editing or enhancing the message. Her delivery style alone makes Michelle unique.

Visiting Michelle is a totally different experience. A high energy atmosphere fills the audience as Michelle talks. She is easy going and comfortable with her topics, effortlessly putting even the most nervous at ease. She provides an intimate, yet sharing experience that's a refreshing change from the usual somber and reserved image created by others who too often pass along simple, generic messages.

*   *   *

Born into an indifferent and inattentive family, Michelle did not have a happy childhood. From a very young age a neighbor often acted as her substitute parent. The neighbor was abusive and involved in the occult. He soon recognized Michelle's gifts and pressured her to develop her psychic skills.

Throughout her childhood, Michelle talked with and took heed of spirits and her own angels. Locals, and other children thought her strange, they were uncomfortable with her early maturity and knowledge, as she seemed to look into their lives. Michelle at that time assumed that everyone else could, like her, talk with the unseen spirits that populated her world.

By mental and physical abuse, the substitute father figure tried to lead Michelle down an alternative pathway. Michelle was saved from that route by daily conversations with her own Guardian Angels who nurtured and protected her from the unhealthy controls forced on her. Eventually, with advancing maturity and the help of prayer and her Guardian Angels, Michelle was released from her childhood traumas.

Eager for more knowledge of the exciting Spirit world she could see, Michelle focused for a few years on everyday religion, and buried herself in the teachings of the Pentecostal Church. Eventually, she came to realize that her insight into the Spirit World didn't need the boundaries of a formal religion. God was everywhere with Michelle. She feels his love and comfort always, and has grown beyond the dogmatic teachings of the church.

Shortly after graduating from high school, Michelle was involved in a serious car accident that killed her cousin and a young friend. She had been warned by her Spirit Guide not to go on that car ride that day, a warning message that she ignored.

Michelle was seriously injured in the accident and died on the pavement as paramedics fought to save her young life. Despite severe internal injuries and massive blood loss they succeeded in restarting her heart and she was brought back to life, but during those intervening minutes she underwent a profound, near death experience. The journey that she made, while in a state of death, caused her to fully recognize her gifts. The near death experience became a changing event in her young life, as she accepted her responsibilities and unique abilities.

Recovered from the accident after a lengthy convalescence, she worked as a cosmetologist in a local beauty salon. She found inspiration at work as she combined her daily work with her love of the Spirit World and relayed messages from her Spirit Guides to customers in the salon.

By that time, Michelle had realized the importance of the Spirit World in her life and she often received messages and advice that helped her in her daily life.

Just two weeks before she was due to marry, she received a troubling message from her Guardian Angel. Forewarned of infidelity, she and her best friend drove the two hundred miles from Miami to Tampa and discovered her fiancé in another woman's arms. This was another important message from her angels to confirm the accuracy and importance of spiritual warnings.

Eventually, she opened her own beauty salon in a small storefront in a Fort Lauderdale suburb. There she was able to relay to her clients messages from the spirit world. After some time, her business underwent a major change. More and more people visited her salon for readings and messages, while her beauty equipment gathered dust.

After a series of deep meditations and self counseling, she decided to close her successful business and concentrate on helping others.

Now Michelle is a professional psychic medium who devotes all her time and energy to helping people communicate with Spirits and Angels. This provides closure to the bereaved and promotes an understanding of the other side of life too many of us ignore. She counsels many people and teaches regularly. Her spiritual lessons are all related to the message of God's unconditional love and mankind's ability to change the world we live in.

Michelle's book conveys a tremendous message of love and inspiration, and I know everyone who reads her book derives the same satisfaction and enjoyment from it as I did, when I first turned the pages. Despite being close to Michelle for many years, I still find something new to learn, from each and every page in this book.

She is truly one of God's messengers on Earth.

Oceans of Love, Shanté Powders

1

WELCOME TO MY WORLD

I am Michelle Whitedove and I welcome you into my world.

I am a medium, psychic, lecturer, teacher, channel and spiritual counselor. Gifted since childhood with the ability to see into the spirit world, I call myself a Light Worker. I believe, my purpose in life is to be a messenger of God.

As a teenager, I was seriously injured in a horrific car crash that claimed the lives of two of my friends. Lying on the pavement, at the side of the wrecked car, I had a near death experience. While in the spirit world, I was told that my mission on Earth is to help people by explaining the spirit world and bringing people into contact with their spiritual selves.

Religions of every credo have some answers, but most of us are too busy or skeptical to follow our religion regularly. It's natural that in times of pain and loss, we turn for comfort and guidance to the religion of our family and our youth.

Yet, all too often we ask questions that religions cannot answer, for they demand 'belief' and acceptance of their word, yet deep down, their help isn't what we want. We want to understand. To understand who we are, why we're here on earth and perhaps what's happened to our lost loved ones. As society changes and becomes more relaxed and open, we are no longer scared by religious tradition and convention. We have the built-in confidence to ask the hard questions and demand answers. Sadly, many of us cannot accept the trite explanations of life and death given by the dogma of older religions.

My message is the same for all races and followers of any religion. All religions are man-made. They follow their own dogma and tradition, but we all pray to the same God.

I especially enjoy working with children. They are light, a complete energy source, a great source of love and pure of spirit. Children represent our future and the next generation of man. They are our nearest living link to the spiritual world and they are still connected to God.

I believe my work on earth will not be complete until I open a special home for abused, abandoned and spiritually damaged children. It will be a healing and spiritual learning center, a safe haven for all children.

*　　*　　*

It's sad, but true, that in today's frenetic, high-speed society most of us are too busy working, bringing up our families and trying to save for a comfortable retirement to ask the fundamental questions about our lives here on Earth.

Too many people drive forward blindly, pre-occupied with the here and now, to stop and think about their spiritual needs. They only pause their frantic rushing around when faced with a crisis in their lives; the serious illness of a family member, the death of a loved one or on hearing of the latest public figure suddenly killed and lost to the world. The deaths of Princess Diana, Mother Theresa and lately, John F. Kennedy Jr. caused millions of people to pause their lives and ask why.

Such dramatic and painful events bring the unprepared to a crashing stop and open up a whole new vista. A world filled with frustrated concern and a lack of understanding that leads to fear and a desperate search for answers.

Faced with emotional crises we all too often find ourselves unable to cope, and it's at such breakpoints in our lives that we may, for the first time question ourselves and what our lives are really all about.

What are we doing here?

And the biggest question, what happens when we die?

More and more people are realizing that there has to be something more. It's inconceivable that we just die and that life finishes when we stop breathing. But where do people turn to find out the truth of what really happens we when die?

Mediums and psychics through the ages have known the truth about life and death and have told those caring to hear. In the last decade as mankind continues its headlong rush into a self-made oblivion there is a great upsurge of people seeking the truth.

The number of people turning to mediums for guidance and an explanation of life and death is growing tremendously and only now for the first time, since the Middle Ages are psychics and mediums being listened to again by the masses.

Recently, I was visited by a lady who had lost her husband in an accident. The last time she saw him, as he left for work, they exchanged harsh words (as often happens.) Later that day her world was turned upside down; her very existence was threatened, when a policeman knocked at her door and broke the terrible news that her husband had been killed in an accident.

Months after the funeral, the lady still couldn't come

to terms with her loss, that she hadn't told her husband she loved him, before he left for the last time.

As soon as I started the reading her husband's spirit approached me. He was smiling, secure in the oneness of the spirit world.

I told the lady that her husband had been with her all the time, through the police interviews, with the medical examiner and the funeral. All the long, lonely nights when she'd sat crying, he had been with her.

Now she was crying, not from her loss and feelings of guilt, but from the love and joy of being temporarily re-united with her husband. She could feel his presence in the room and took comfort from his messages.

The husband passed messages about other members of their family, stories I couldn't have possibly known because I didn't know the lady or her family history.

At the end of the reading she was able to come to terms with her loss and knew that her husband was still alive and well in spirit. She knew that they would one day be together, again. Now she can get on with her life and enjoy the moments yet to come, and nurture and support their young children.

The experiences of that lady are not unique. We can all contact spirits; we all have angels and spirit guides that will help us. We have to be receptive and open our minds and hearts with love and prayer.

In this book I attempt to introduce you, the reader, to the spiritual world of God and his helpers, explain the transition between this life and what we call death, and demonstrate that the spirit world is all around us. I will show you how to recognize God's helpers for what they truly are.

There is a new dawn in the air; an era of enlightenment is coming. It's time to put aside our cynicism and turn to face God, recognize him and understand the teachings of his messengers. Only then will people find peace, love and serenity

So, take the journey with me as I explain what the spirit world is all about.

*The LORD chooses messengers
from among the Angels
and from men.*

– The Koran

CHAPTER

2

MY NEAR DEATH EXPERIENCE

*A*s far back as can I remember in my childhood, I was always aware of angels and spirits, I accepted them as a normal part of life. In my inexperience and youth, I assumed that everyone else could see and talk with their angels as easily as I did.

As I grew older I soon came to realize that many of my peers thought I was a little bit strange, as I told them about my unseen friends. Adults tended to ignore my stories as an overactive imagination and chuckled at my 'imaginary' friends.

Nevertheless, I continued talking and communicating with my spirit guides throughout my childhood, and I took a lot of comfort from the sure knowledge that I was never alone. I was seldom scared of unusual situations or the nighttime darkness in my bedroom.

As I grew into a teenager, I was still aware of my spirit guides, unlike many teens I was never rebellious, in fact I spent a lot of my teenage years conversing with my spiritual friends. From time to time they visited me and relayed warnings of potential danger.

While still a teenager I underwent a life changing event, an experience that was to alter the whole course of my life.

I was eighteen and had recently graduated high school, it was early July and the weather was extremely hot, and I was enjoying the holiday celebrations.

In the afternoon, on Sunday, July 6th, I was at the Volusia County Speedway with my family and some friends. As the long day passed, we all became hot and tired. After a lot of cajoling I agreed to accompany them on a trip to a nearby shopping mall to hang out for a while.

Five of us piled into my cousin's old car and we headed off to the mall. Unaccountably, I felt apprehensive and knew I shouldn't be making the journey.

But I considered myself invincible, I was sure I knew everything there was to know about life, such is the ego of an average teenager.

I sat in my usual seat, next to the driver. I felt nervous and suddenly shouted at her to stop the car! I said I wanted to sit in the back and traded my seat with a fourteen-year-old friend, who was keen to take a place up front. I climbed into the back of the car, sitting between my cousin and another friend. I didn't know it then, but in that instant, we had just swapped lives.

As we were driving along the highway I wasn't paying much attention; I was focusing on some photographs on my knees. The car was full of noisy happy kids, as we drove along in the hot summer afternoon.

Suddenly, a dog ran out in front of the car and my cousin who was driving instinctively swerved away. Panicked, she unknowingly veered into the path of an oncoming van.

I'd been unaware of any problems, it all happened so fast, but I remember the scream and the motion as the car swerved violently. I looked up from the pictures just in time to see the dog dart across the two-lane highway. The van collided head on into our car.

Within a split second, I smashed face first into the back of the front seat and was then thrown back with an explosive force. Bleeding and badly injured, I was knocked unconscious.

The next thing I remember, I was lying on the pavement. I knew I was severely injured, with a smashed face and the feel of a crushing weight on my chest - a weight so heavy that I couldn't breathe. I felt a deep intense pain in my back and instinctively knew my spine was broken. My arm was twisted at an impossible angle and I could see that it was also badly broken.

I realized that I was dying. Lying on a roadside on the Fourth of July weekend, bleeding to death and nearly leaving the world behind me, the pain was so intense I prayed to God to take me and let me die.

As I lay there looking up at the sky I felt my energy draining away, my life force was leaving my body as I slipped towards death. Gradually, a feeling of serenity seeped through me and I felt content. The pain seemed to ease away and suddenly I realized I was floating above my body.

It was a strange moment. Seconds before I'd been unable to breathe and locked in great agonizing pain, yet now I could look down at myself lying on the roadside, watching almost unemotionally as my lifeblood pooled under my body.

I thought I was dead. I looked around and realized that I was just the same as I'd been an instant before the crash. I was uninjured and able to move easily, I was just a lighter version of myself. Looking down at my wrecked former body I was glad to leave it behind.

I could see the paramedics working frantically on my body and I distinctly heard one of them say, "Hurry, we're losing her."

Their frenetic rushing seemed distant and unimportant. I floated above the accident scene for what seemed a long long, time, but in reality could only have been minutes. Intuitively, I knew that some had died in the crash, but it didn't seem too important for I knew that what came after death was better than the life we lived before.

Suddenly, I became aware of a bright white light higher above me. I looked up and felt a pull towards the light. I heard gentle soothing voices and felt a tremendous energy all around me. The light was so bright it was shimmering and a great wave of love washed over me. It was a perfect feeling, like nothing I'd ever experienced during my life on Earth.

Curious and eager, I turned towards the light and started to move towards it, intent on joining with the feelings of peace and love.

Suddenly, I felt a familiar presence and heard the voices of my Guardian Angels, voices I'd heard many times as a child.

It wasn't my time they told me, I had to go back, for I had work to do on Earth. The messages came like waves and filled my mind. I had to go back and live out a life on Earth, I had much work to do and an important mission to complete.

I clearly remember feeling disappointed and cheated that I couldn't yet go to the light and join them. I argued that I was content and wanted to go home with them, I knew that there was something better on the other side of the bright white light. I refused to go back to earth, not that I ever had any choice in the matter.

They sent me back, but made a concession. I told them I was afraid of the terrible pain and damage to my body, I was sure that my back was broken and I would be crippled for the rest of my life on earth. With love and concern in their voices, they promised to alleviate the pain. Somehow I knew I would have a rapid recovery and be able to fulfill my earthbound mission; I was destined to help people, to be a messenger and spread the word about the spirit world to all that would listen.

So, reluctantly, I returned to my body. I was very upset at being sent back. I looked down at myself once more and saw the paramedics still doing their best to coax life back into my unresponsive body - at least they would be happy I thought.

My next thoughts were in a hospital emergency room. I awoke to hear the car driver, my cousin, screaming on the table next to me, so I knew she was alive too. A nurse shaved my head while another pushed in a large needle. They sent me off into a narcotic induced sleep.

Much later, I found out my full list of injuries; right arm shattered, broken ankle, broken spine, severe blood loss and internal injuries from impact, damaged lungs, bruised heart muscle and a smashed face completed the picture. Everyone in the hospital thought it a miracle I'd survived the accident.

Unconscious and very weak, I was put on a ventilator in the Intensive Care Unit. Doctors told my family they doubted if I'd last the next twenty-four hours because of the extent of my injuries, but if I did then I'd probably make a complete recovery.

My prayers had been answered. My angels helped me through the pain; I went into a lengthy period of suspended animation, without pain or dreams - just a blessed nothingness, as my body started the long healing process.

After about ten days of unconsciousness, I awoke and learned the death toll of that horrific crash. Both my cousin, who was seated next to me and the fourteen year old boy who traded places with me had died of their injuries.

Despite a heavy heart and sadness at the sudden and tragic passing of my two friends, I made a quick physical recovery. I underwent more operations and ended up with metal pins in the broken arm and ankle.

To the amazement of my doctors, my face healed completely without any need for major re-constructive surgery, except maybe a slight crook in my nose. That was a small price to pay for an opportunity to see the other side of the veil, and come back and tell the world what really awaits us on the other side.

My experience with such a passage through the veil of life, altered my life forever. Now I knew that all my childhood visitors were real and weren't just figments of my imagination. There was a whole universe waiting patiently for us. I would never ignore any warning messages from my angels and spirit guides again.

Suddenly I was grown up, and I knew my real purpose in life; I was to tell people about my certain knowledge of the spirit world.

God sends forth guardians
who watch over you and
carry away your soul without fail
when death over takes you.

– The Koran

DEATH – A COMING HOME PARTY

A great deal of my work as a spiritualist is connected with events surrounding the passing from this life into the spirit world. I spend countless hours explaining to people who have lost a loved one or good friend what really happens when we die.

Death is the single most feared event in the life of all humans. From the moment of our birth, when the soul enters our bodies, the clock starts ticking. The seconds, minutes and hours start counting up until the inevitable end of this life - death.

Death comes in a variety of guises, old age, through sickness, following accidents, murder and suicide. At the time of our death, the way of our passing is not too important. But know this, the experience is one of our own choosing.

We die whether we've lived a good life or bad, whether we're young or old - when that time comes for each of us, we will surely cease breathing and we will die.

For every one of us the toil, worry and fears of life are taken away at the point of death as we fall back limply, our bodies just a shell whose soul has departed. The physical body is simply the container that hosts our soul for the years of life on Earth.

Many people fear death, they fear it for themselves and for their loved ones. Mothers and fathers, wives, husbands, brothers, sisters, dear friends - each has to let go at the point of death for they cannot help their loved one to cross from life into death, nor can they prevent that passing.

I don't believe death is an event to be feared, nor do I believe we should be unduly saddened by the death of another, even a loved one who we held dear to our hearts.

But what happens during and after those final moments?

As a medium, I've spoken with many, many spirits that have left their earthly life behind them and now inhabit the spirit world. Each spirit has their own story to tell. Those stories alone would fill a library of books, but they all have the same feelings about the moment of death.

There is a sense of drifting away. Pain subsides and then stops, soon to be forgotten. Worries and earthly concerns become more distant and seem to be at arms length, consciousness changes, then we see and move on a different plane of existence.

Some of the departed feel the presence of their guardian angels before the actual moment of death, they see them in the room, feel their presence or a sense of warmth and love washes over them.

This feeling of warmth and love sometimes leaves a mark on a person just at the point of death. How often do people comment when they view the earthly remains of a loved one, "He never looked as good in life as he does now. He looks peaceful and at rest."

Sometimes, people who lie on the brink of death, at home or in a hospital bed comment that they can see and talk with deceased partners or relatives.

"Here's Aunt Sally, can you see her?" is an often asked question, by someone about to die.

Of course we cannot see Aunt Sally, but the person about to pass over can. Spirit guides are present for the one about to die and they are doing a great and loving duty, they have manifested themselves to ease the fear of dying. The spirits reveal themselves so that the person about to die knows there are better things awaiting them; they comfort and assist them with the transition from this earthly life, through the transition and into the spirit world.

We, the sad relatives simply believe that our poor

relative is rambling, hallucinating, as he, or she succumbs to strong medication and imminent death. We cannot see what they see, for we are still firmly rooted in the present, the here and now, that will soon cease to exist for our loved one.

When the body stops breathing and shuts down for the last time, then the earthly shell is spent and dead. The body has no further use (unless for organ donations) and can be buried or cremated, it has served its purpose as an earthly container for the soul, a soul that has now departed for the spirit world.

Finally the eyes close for that last time; the Silver Cord severs and the soul is released from the body. The Silver Cord is a sort of unseen, to our eyes, umbilical cord that fastens the soul to the human body, when broken, the soul is no longer tied to the body and can float away - free of its earthbound constraints.

Once the soul floats away from the body, it may hover just above the body for a while as their spirit guides and Guardian Angels gather around and guide the soul to the start of its next journey. Spirits sometimes linger for days, even to the point of watching their own funeral. The reason they do this should be fully understood.

The lingering of the soul after death helps those left behind, giving the family and friends time to come to terms with their grief and loss and allows the spirit a time to say goodbye to those who were loved during the time on earth.

Sometimes spirits visit loved ones when the person is asleep; they visit in dreamtime and say their goodbyes either just before their physical death or just after the event.

When this period is over, and all earthly tasks are completed the spirit is content to move into the light and continue its own journey of evolution.

So the death that we see is really just the starting point of another journey for the soul. A timeless journey that each of us has to make at some pre-ordained time.

Our soul, complete with all the stored information about our lives - the choices we made, the good and bad things we have done, the wishes and ambitions, still has a choice.

The soul needs to travel into the pure white light that waits for us all in the celestial world. The white light has many different names, but the light represents all that is good, unconditional love and God. We must travel into that light before we complete our journey.

Our Guardian Angels assist our souls passage, but don't force us, for we still have our own will and the ability to make choices. Nothing is more important than that our soul makes the right choice and chooses to turn and go into the light, for only then do we complete our journey and move into the next stage of our spiritual life.

The soul has a memory. Our thoughts, our deeds, our beliefs, personality, and our mind are imprinted on our soul. So when we die we're simply a 'lighter' version of who we were just before death came to us.

We remember the ones we left on earth, we feel their pain and loss and we take the memories of life with us as we journey into the light. We are happy to be going home again to paradise in the heavens, where all is perfect.

I know I've made that journey several times, yet I still find it difficult to describe the awesome sense of radiating warmth, understanding, forgiveness, wisdom and love that washes over the soul as we enter the light.

Once the soul enters the light, the last vestiges of the earthly life are truly over and the soul has once again come back home into Heaven, united as a member of the celestial universe, above and beyond the cares and worries of the human race.

In my experience death is not an event to be feared; though, it is a time of sadness. Sadness for the life partner or loved one we have lost, we will never again in this life hear the voice or the laughter we know and love so much.

Many people miss the companionship and the sharing after the passing of a loved one, but sometimes that loss is tinged with a sense of loneliness and self-pity, as the remaining partners feel cheated of their best friend by death. When we grieve our lost loved one it is the natural process. But when we continue to grieve for extended periods of time we hinder the growth of our loved one on the other side. Our thoughts of sorrow and longing constantly pull on their spirit. We distract them from their continued spiritual path.

It is only right and natural that we feel sadness at the loss of a friend and lover, but even in our sadness we should be thankful that our dead loved one has not ceased to exist, they have simply moved on to a different, better, plane of existence. In time we shall be re-united, if we wish, with our lost friends and partners, and we should take comfort from knowing that they are with us and will certainly be there to help us when our turn comes to move towards the light.

Life is a continuing process and our time on earth is but a snapshot of our soul's existence throughout eternity.

*   *   *

I remember helping a middle aged man come to terms with his wife's impending death. His story was deeply disturbing and his fortitude impressed me greatly.

Mr. Taylor came to see me for a private reading. As soon as we sat down I sensed a great sadness and feeling of impending loss around the man. He told me his wife was very sick and unable to attend a joint reading.

As I connected with the spirit world I knew what ailed her and I knew that the lady wasn't just sick, she was terminally ill. As is my way, I told Mr. Taylor of her physical problems and told him that she would soon die. I felt her pain and a great sense of tiredness washed over me. She was nearly finished, tired of fighting the cancer that was steadily eating her body. Her energy was very weak and I felt she'd already given up the lost fight and wanted to go home to the spirit world.

There's no easy way to tell a stranger that a loved one is going to die soon, and Mr. Taylor was no exception. I sat there and comforted him as his heart was breaking.

After giving the sad message from the spirit world I knew that I had to counsel Mr. Taylor. I explained to him the transition between this life we have and the spirit world. I prepared him for the coming loss and explained that death was not an end, only a change, and that we shouldn't grieve for the one that we've lost here, for we will surely meet again in the heavens. A world that knows no pain, only love and understanding.

I told Mr. Taylor that his wife was moving on to a better place and that she would be happier once she'd crossed the veil into the spirit world, leaving her pain and suffering behind on earth.

A few weeks later Mr. Taylor visited me again. He was planning to take his wife to a clinic for experimental medical therapy, a plan that would entail a long journey as well as costing several thousand dollars.

In spirit again, I saw that his wife had weakened considerably since his last visit. I could see her death coming very soon, there was nothing that anyone could do on this earth to save her life. The most he could hope for was to take an extension of time before her death, but such an extension could be cruel and pain filled for her.

Sadly, I had to tell Mr. Taylor that his wife, a lady he loved dearly and treated like a princess, would probably not survive the long trip to a different clinic. She was too weak and her time on earth was very nearly finished.

The hardest part of meeting with Mr. Taylor was that I knew his wife's pain was being drawn out by her love for her husband. She knew she was going to die and wanted to go on, but her love for her husband was holding her back, keeping her in this life.

Many times people who are ready to leave this life hold on, because they don't want to cause grief and suffering for their loved ones.

Mr. Taylor wanted to know how he could help his wife; he would have done anything to help. I took his hand and gently explained that he had to give her his blessing and allow her to move on to the next world.

I explained that at the moment of her death the pain would cease and she would travel upward and enter back into the spirit world, for her soul it would be a time of celebration. People who pass on are greeted by their friends, loved ones and family who have passed on earlier. There is no blackness, just an outpouring of love that suffuses the soul.

I talked and counseled Mr. Taylor for a long time, and when he was mentally prepared, I told him when his wife would die. Very upset, but fortified by my revelations of what would happen to his wife's soul after death, he went home to spend some final time with her.

Weeks later, he called to thank me for my help and advice and told me his wife had died within three days of the date I'd given him. Though sad at her loss, he told me that they'd talked about her passing and he realized that she wasn't afraid of death, but that she had been sad at the thought of leaving him alone. They talked about meeting again on the other side of this life and soon thereafter, Mr. Taylor's wife slipped peacefully from this life and into the next.

*   *   *

Unlike Mrs. Taylor's death, death doesn't always visit when we're terminally sick and when we've mentally readied ourselves for dying.

Death visits people by way of accidents and violence too. Then our bodies are damaged and broken beyond repair with a suddenness that gives us no warning. But our angels are always with us, waiting at our side for whenever we need them.

I remember helping a couple whom had lost a son in sudden, tragic circumstances. They asked me to help them with a joint reading.

Normally, I only give readings for one person at a time. Sometimes there are risks associated with readings for couples; secrets, infidelities and other matters can come out into the open and turn a reading into a pitched battle.

I told the couple about my concerns about a joint reading, but they were adamant; they wanted to make contact with someone from the spirit world - they weren't seeking marriage counseling!

I agreed to see them and they duly appeared on time a few days later, a friendly middle-aged couple called Peterson.

Once they were seated and relaxed, I sat down with

them and told them how I work. I pray and meditate and ask my guardian angels and spirit guides for assistance. I also ask any souls coming from love and light that may want to contact the client to come forward. Most often I get through to the right spirit, but sometimes another soul comes forward; there cannot be any guarantees when communing with the spirit world. You don't always get who you want to contact, but you do get who you need. God knows what is in our best interest. It is a blessing and a gift to receive a message from the otherside.

I always ask clients to reinforce my requests by praying to their guides and angels at the same time.

While I was praying for the Petersons, a strong presence very quickly came forward and made itself known to me. The spirit was forceful and almost impatient, as if it had been just waiting for an opportunity to communicate. It was a clean shaven, handsome young man in his early twenties with short black hair, I acknowledged him and noticed that he was dressed in some sort of military uniform. He was smiling at me.

I described the spirit in some detail and the Petersons confirmed that he was the spirit they wished to contact, yes, I was describing their son, who had died suddenly while in the army. Tears welled up in the mother's eyes and flowed unchecked down her cheeks, she was both sad and deliriously happy at the same time.

I knew then that their son had brought them here to see me, so that he could get his message to them.

He was happy to see them, and he told me he was happy now back in the spirit world, I related this and saw relief wash over the parents.

Suddenly, I saw the manner of the boy's death. He was driving a large heavy-duty truck, I saw artillery, guns and shells, a great explosion - that was how he had died.

The father handed me a photo of a young man in military clothing, it was the spirit I could see and feel. The Petersons knew I was in direct contact with their son, and they were very grateful.

I told them that their son was happy, that though it had been his time to go. He wanted them to know that his time on earth was supposed to have been short. He died serving his country, and he was happy to die in such an honorable manner, they shouldn't be sad for him.

The young man told me there was some confusion about his death. He wanted his parents to know that it wasn't his fault, another soldier with him knew the truth.

The parents were amazed, they confirmed that their son had been killed in the army and that his death was shrouded in suspicion and secrecy, and the army had blamed him for his own death.

The boy's spirit told me that his friend knew the truth, but that his family was to put the matter behind them and get on with their lives. Now that they knew the truth of his death, he was at peace. He told me they would all meet again, in the future.

When the reading ended, both the mother and father were crying with joyous relief and love for their dead son. They felt they too could let their son go now. They would always love him and remember him, but now they felt they could finally stop grieving for his sudden passing.

Death Date

Know that we don't have one pre-destined date upon which we will die. All of us have a choice of dates of death, determined by our spiritual progress at a particular time in our soul's evolution.

In this way we can suffer serious accidents or illnesses and yet have apparently miraculous recoveries, or we can have a close call with death, by accident or illness.

In reality there are no close calls or miraculous recoveries. The extension of our life is decided by God. We continue to live out this life because we still have unfinished business and missions to accomplish.

When death does visit us, it sometimes comes without warning; the Silver Cord is severed and the soul is released from the body. The soul carries our mind, and the mind can be in shock - unprepared for the sudden turn of events.

Our celestial 'lighter' self sometimes fails to understand or come to grips with the new consciousness and that's when our guardian angels are invaluable, we need them to guide us the right way - toward the light.

When a soul is suddenly released from a physical body the mind can be confused and still feel earthly emotions. Experienced as a sense of loss, a need to visit a partner, children or parents aren't unusual thoughts.

Feelings of frustration, money problems, revenge, worry, obligations crowd together and confuse the soul. This can be dangerous, for the negative vibrations counter the efforts of our angels and spirit guides. In this confusion the soul can be delayed from entering the white light temporarily or even become wayward for many years as a "ghost".

CHAPTER

4

GHOSTS, POLTERGEISTS AND EXORCISMS

Some souls, especially after a violent death, refuse to enter the light and remain earthbound. This in between stage of earthly death and the spiritual world can last for many years.

The soul cannot return to life in the body it just departed. It simply cannot turn back the clock and pick up the pieces where life stopped.

Yet, until the soul enters 'The Light' and re-joins the spirit world, it is doomed to exist between the two planes in a middle zone, fixed on the earth, but invisible and unable to participate in human life.

These earthbound, or wayward spirits, are what we know as ghosts.

It is important that we don't confuse ghosts with our Spirit Guides. Spirit Guides are the ancient spirits that act as our spiritual helpers. They are from the celestial universe to help and guide us in our lives, and after our death.

There are many reports of people in times of

imminent life threatening danger when 'ghosts' have appeared before them and warned them of approaching danger. Those ghosts were actually the person's Spirit Guides, they have a special linkage with us and are in place to assist us. Ghosts do not have that special empathy with the living.

As earthbound spirits they have not yet made the journey into the light, they have no peace and they can still maintain earthly ambitions and desires.

Some ghosts are kindly and some are not - just as in life we find some good and some bad personality types in people.

Generally, any manifestation or apparition from the spiritual world is a truly frightening event for most humans. A ghost represents something we don't understand. It is ethereal and different, it may look similar to someone we once knew, but generally people who see an earthbound spirit, even of a relative or friend, are frightened.

Sometimes, a ghost will stay in places or near people they are familiar with, which is why some ghosts are associated with particular buildings or locations.

During the Battle of the Somme in the Great War of 1914-18 more than 40,000 soldiers were killed by the end of the first bloody day. Waves of foot soldiers attacked the German trenches over open ground and were cut down by a wall of machine gun fire.

Today, the Somme, a small agricultural village in northern France, is a recognized area where ghosts still linger to this day. The ghosts are the souls of the young allied soldiers, suddenly killed as they ran forward towards the enemy, running side by side with their comrades in arms, their souls forcibly ejected from their broken and smashed bodies.

Little wonder that these souls are unhappy, lost, and confused. So they continue to haunt their last associations with their earthly lives, unable to believe in their own deaths and such a tragic waste of life.

I know that eventually all those souls will find peace as they turn to the light and enter the Kingdom of Heaven.

Ghosts frequently live in or occupy buildings in which they feel comfortable. If the current human occupants of a home or building are comfortable sharing their quarters with a ghost, then no harm will occur. This is not an uncommon occurrence and is harmless to the human and ghost occupants. Unfortunately, while the spirit may share the occupancy for a time (sometimes many years) that does not mean that eventually the spirit has to give up its hold on the place and move into the celestial world.

Clearing and Blessing

Often clients ask me to perform a clearing and blessing for their home or business. I have cleared ghosts; poltergeists and negative energies that hang onto the places people inhabit. Clearing these lower vibrations from a building can make a difference in daily life.

A few months ago, I read for a very interesting lady, she was looking for a location to open an antique shop. I told her the location would be on a main street surrounded by other businesses, with a restaurant next door.

This location seemed important to me and I told her to keep my advice in mind because that location would guarantee people walking by the store window.

Three months later, she called me again. She had taken my advice and found the location that I'd spoken of and had settled into her new storefront for five weeks.

But people weren't coming inside the store, many people would stop and window shop, but not many actually went inside.

From the conversation, I picked up that an unsuccessful business had been in that same location and left behind negative energy caused by the failure. It needed to be removed. I told her the news and quickly set up a time to clear and bless her new business.

The day arrived and as I entered the premises I could tell this was supposed to be a thriving business. The place was full of natural light and the floor plan was open. We were surrounded by the most beautiful antiques, nevertheless I could feel a heaviness - negative energy left over from the last business.

As I started clearing and blessing I could feel the energy transform. As I was finishing the blessing, the lady client was surprised when a couple came to the door and asked if they could come in, the store wasn't to be open for another hour.

She invited them in and they immediately walked over to a twenty-three thousand dollar chandelier. I finished my work and left. Later in the evening she called to thank me again, she had sold the chandelier and there had been more people in the store that day than the entire five weeks that she had been open.

*   *   *

Unfortunately, not all earthbound spirits or energies are so harmless. Some souls hold a lot of anger and rage, and they can cause problems for those of us still in this physical world.

If a tragic event, such as a murder or suicide, occurs in a place and a soul is literally thrown out of a living body then an imprint of the event can be forced into the ethereal matter of the room. This event leaves a mark or scar on time and space.

The tragic scene replays night after night, like a hologram, a transparent physical manifestation that we can see. We are watching a replay of the imprint on the room, eventually the imprint will fade away and cease.

*   *   *

Children sometimes re-visit us as ghosts. Young and confused, they are inevitably impish ghosts that do no harm; they're simply living out the childhood that was denied them in life. Most often they stay attached to a familiar place. Once they bore of their limbo existence, they go into the light. Their innocence gives them a glow that is warming for everyone who witnesses a child's apparition.

Poltergeists

Poltergeists are a special type of earthbound spirit or soul. They are restless souls who have no peace. Invariably, poltergeists are spirits that were snatched from life and they refuse to relinquish their hold on the physical life.

They harbor earthly emotions such as revenge, the need for justice, hate, addiction cravings, intolerance and just plain rage. A person with such negativity in this life could be a perfect candidate for an earthbound spirit after death. These strong negative emotions tug on the just deceased, the remembrance and emotions it feels can give it reason to stay earthbound thus creating a poltergeist.

A poltergeist will sometimes try to attach itself to a vulnerable human to absorb their living energy or light. For example: A hard core alcoholic hanging out at a local bar can attract to himself a wayward spirit with similar addictions or cravings. In this way, a dark spirit will attach itself to a human to soak up the feeling of alcohol. Once these spirits attach themselves, they influence the earthly host to continually drink. Without knowing why, the human tends to go from bad to worse, bingeing on drugs, and alcohol, getting violent and talking incoherently, moving in a downward spiral, unless an exorcism is performed.

Poltergeists can manifest themselves to us, and some even have enough power to cause change in the physical world. They can move or even throw objects, pictures, pots and pans and so on. They have even been known to topple heavy furniture and open and close doors.

They seem to delight in frightening people who they target, sometimes violently so. They also have the ability to create smells and noises that have no real basis in real-time events.

If a poltergeist invades a house and chooses to reside there, then often the only way to remove them is by the power of exorcism.

Exorcisms

I have practiced exorcisms for several years; today, I only exorcise spirits where a child is involved. Exorcism is a method by which especially violent or angry souls are driven from a specific location, building or person.

Exorcisms are not pleasant events; they are the excluding of a dead person's soul or a dark spirit from a place or person by a ritualistic method, a method that includes meditation, ritual, prayer and the assistance of the Archangel Michael and God.

It is imperative that the person conducting the exorcism has tremendous faith in God, their Angels, and themselves to successfully accomplish an exorcism.

The exorcist has to be confident in his or her abilities and stand his or her ground when confronting the wayward spirit. I believe my success at exorcising negative spirits is because I am in close contact with Archangel Michael and I frequently call on him to assist me.

My angels show the poor lost spirit the way to the light and assist their passage. Once the spirit leaves the location where it is not welcome and turns towards the light, then the exorcism has been successfully concluded. Even so, if the poltergeist sees the light, then having it's own free will it can refuse to enter, and then the exorcist must be content with simply removing the spirit from a specific location or person.

Sometimes a spirit locks onto a living person's aura. Wayward spirits can be attracted to children because of their soul's bright light. The wayward literally invades the child's body; this is called a Possession.

Possessions demand immediate exorcism because the well being or life of the child can be at stake.

The wayward spirit invades the human host and takes possession of the body. Sometimes a child host will adopt an adult voice and mannerisms, abusing and swearing at others who threaten the spirit. Similarly the child will display adult strength and physically attack others, especially those who attempt to exorcise the spirit from the child's body.

Such exorcisms must be conducted in strict accordance with the ancient rituals, and it's often necessary to have helpers available to physically restrain a spitting, swearing, fighting child controlled by a poltergeist, until the exorcism is complete.

I vividly recall a possession I was asked to deal with by a distraught mother called Tina.

Initially, she came to me for a reading, looking for help and insight into her nine year old's behavioral problems. Doctors had put him on mood altering drugs to try and make him more normal, but she was looking for the root causes of his problems.

Her son refused to sleep in his own room, he was very anti-social, rebelling and was vindictive towards both parents. His personality seemed to change from normal to violent without reason or warning.

Using my psychic skills, I could see clearly there was a male entity around him, it was dark and manipulative. I told Tina that a clearing and blessing was needed to rid the house and her son of the spirit. Tina felt that the doctors were not making any progress treating her son and realized that the situation demanded a more radical solution; she was willing to have her house blessed.

When I arrived, Tina had sent her family out for the afternoon. As I walked through the house, I could feel a dense, heavy, negative force. It was even stronger in the boy's bedroom. The heavy vibrations confirmed my worst fears. I knew without a doubt that the spirit had attached itself to the boy.

I cleared and blessed the house and then told the mother I needed to see her son. I knew that an exorcism needed to be performed to remove the dark entity.

On the day of the exorcism I called on Archangel Michael, the protector of our souls. I thanked him for removing this spirit from the child.

As I approached the child, he backed away from me. I could see the tall dark man that was with him and he wanted nothing to do with me, recognizing me as a threat, for he recognized me as a light worker for God.

During the ceremony, the dark entity resisted, the boy could see him and worked to free himself. At one point, while separating the boy from the wayward spirit, he said, "He needs more salt." Salt is used as a protective agent.

With much faith in God, my Angels and guides, I was successful in removing the entity from the boy and the house. The spirit did not go to the light, but it was no longer allowed to be with this child.

Days later, Tina called to thank me. There had been a dramatic difference in her son. He now sleeps in his own room and is once again a loving child.

Amazed, Tina relayed what her son had said to her, "Mommy, did you see the man leave? He walked out the corner of the living room."

***His Angels guard those who
honor the Lord
and rescues them from danger.***

– Psalms 34:7

GHOSTS CREATED BY MEN

*M*an's inhumanity to man is not limited to distant history and today's third world dictatorships. We create our destinies because of the choices we make, sometimes men take the wrong paths and visit tremendous wrong on their fellow man.

One such example occurred in the early days of the United States of America.

During the Native American Indian wars in Colorado a battle was fought between the U.S. Cavalry and a tribe of Indians. With superior arms and more men the Cavalry won the day, after bitter fighting that left many dead on both sides.

The women and children of the tribe were defenseless, left to tend their camps while the Indian braves had gone off to do battle.

The victorious Cavalry sought them out after the battle and discovered their camps.

The federal government decreed that the remaining Indians, mostly women and children were to be moved to a reservation.

It was winter at that time and survivors were lacking food and warmth. It was obvious that the journey to the reservation would kill many of the Indians, so the cavalry in a show of humanity, issued them woolen blankets for the journey.

History shows that it was an intentional act on the part of the government to provide blankets that were infected with the smallpox virus; the women and children were each handed a death warrant in the form of a charitable act.

As the long tiring journey continued, hundreds of the women, their children and babies died of Smallpox on the trail to the reservation. The manner of their dying was particularly painful, the effects of the deadly disease exacerbated by their cold, hunger and fear.

Now many of the dead remain earthbound, their spirits still linger along the route from their camp to the reservation, waiting for their menfolk to return and liberate them from their suffering. The ghosts of the poor souls were frequently seen wandering aimlessly, earthbound, waiting for release from their suffering.

As humanitarians, we can only wonder why a defeated and defenseless group of women and children were ripped from their homes and sent on a forced journey through a cold Colorado winter, their only protection from the weather being deadly infected blankets.

Has society now progressed to a level that such atrocities could not be repeated?

Unfortunately not, the actions of tyrants like Saddam Hussein, the Iraqi dictator who ordered deadly nerve gas attacks against his own defenseless people, demonstrate too well that man has an infinite capacity for cruelty to his fellow man. As a race, mankind hasn't made much progress toward God, tolerance or understanding.

Indeed, despite our apparent progress in society, man still has the cruel ability to kill his brothers and sisters, and those actions themselves create ghosts. Wars, aggression and deranged dictators supply a never ending stream of ghosts to populate the empty battlefields and war torn areas of our world.

War, in the name of God, has been a popular theme for wanton cruelty throughout history and still continues to this day, as men kill each other, supposedly in God's name.

CHAPTER

6

DEATH OF AN ICON

As a medium, I receive messages from many spirits, most of whom were ordinary folk during their life on Earth, but sometimes I talk to the spirits of once famous icons in the public consciousness of the twentieth century.

Famous people play a role both in this world and in spirit. They are more spiritually accountable to God than just normal people, because as famous personalities, celebrities or politicians they have a great influence on massive numbers of ordinary people. Their media exposure, in the press and on television, means that their messages are carried to millions globally and they are looked upon as role models for countless numbers of younger, and sometimes older, people.

Such popular figures lead good lives and demonstrate a great capacity for love, compassion, sympathy and understanding. The are a living demonstration of the way we should all lead our lives.

Many of these popular figures host old souls, full

of love and wisdom, they chose to be with us for a specific purpose.

Some examples of popular figures that have had an influence on our world include:

John F. Kennedy, Jr.

John F. Kennedy, Jr., his wife and sister-in-law were killed when their light plane crashed into the Atlantic Ocean. The young trio was flying to Martha's Vineyard to attend the wedding of a family member. Their sudden, inexplicable death touched and saddened the whole of the United States of America.

Their deaths caused a great outpouring of spontaneous love and sympathy. People that never knew them in life visited their homes and left flowers, messages and lit candles in their honor.

Their passing caused people everywhere to stop and ask, "What is it all about?"

Such events raise the consciousness and provoke thoughts about life and death in ordinary people.

John F. Kennedy, Jr., Caroline and Lauren died for a specific purpose at a pre-ordained time. John was placed in this world to fulfill a mission, not only as a politician like his father, but to demonstrate the power of good and compassion.

The three people had made a pledge in spirit, they agreed before they came to this world to leave it on that day, all together.

John Junior had completed his mission, and both his death, and the form of his passing, were intended to make a statement to the world... "Pay attention, humanitarians are dying amongst you all."

Nobody notices when ordinary Joe Smith, gets killed in a drive-by shooting, a car wreck or any other accident. But a high profile, multiple death grabs worldwide attention, as the whole grisly episode is played out on every news television and radio network.

The death of the trio was another warning, another wake up call for mankind - a message that we ignore at our own peril.

Princess Diana

Princess Diana, the Rose of England, died in tragic circumstances. An inexplicable, late night car crash in Paris, France led to her death.

The circumstances of Princess Diana's death were similar to my near death experience. Diana survived the car crash and like me, she had a near death experience. The difference was that I was told I had to return to this world and live out my life, while Diana had her life review and was given the choice whether to return or not.

Princess Diana chose to remain in spirit, and hence her physical body died in the emergency room of a Paris clinic. She had accomplished her given mission on Earth as a humanitarian, she felt she could do more to help mankind from the spirit world from that time onward. Diana was concerned about the welfare of her two sons, the princes, William and Harry, but she was reassured by her Guardian Angels that they would be fine; Diana, even in death, put mankind before her own needs and desires.

Ostensibly living a fairytale life, Princess Diana did not always have the happy carefree life portrayed by the media. She endured personal hardships, but still managed to help others. Always hounded by the cynical paparazzi in life, even they recognized her compassionate nature and ability to share and help those less fortunate. She helped raise awareness and the need for love. Diana worked particularly well with children, the sick and the needy.

Even the tragic timing of her death, just as she was about to announce to the world her new love, was calculated to give people cause to consider her life.

Her death was a catalyst to millions of people around the world. Strangers by the thousands wrote letters or visited her homes and Buckingham Palace in England to pay tribute to her life. Pop songs were written and sold by the millions, with all the income being given to Diana's favorite charities.

Even in death she did good works that benefited many needy people around the world.

*   *   *

Princess Diana visited me in spirit and asked me to pray for her children, she was concerned with their well being and wanted them to lead normal lives, and not be hounded by the paparazzi.

Sometime later, while teaching in a workshop I was giving a public reading to a lady. I realized that the spirit talking to me was Princess Diana, she was asking me to tell the lady to continue to pray for William and Harry.

Since then, I have discovered that Diana visits other mediums asking for their prayers. She asks highly evolved spiritual souls to pray for her sons because she knows that those individuals have powerful prayers, and that their prayers will protect and nurture her sons.

Mother Theresa

Mother Theresa was a nun who worked in underdeveloped countries helping the sick and starving. Her life was devoted to helping abandoned, orphaned and starving children in the slums of third world cities.

She was devoted to her spiritual work and bringing the world's attention to focus on the desperate plight of the poor and underprivileged, those abandoned and cast aside by society.

Mother Theresa was a mother for all of humanity, she was a living Spirit Guide serving all of us.

Her works received much public acclaim, despite her never seeking publicity. She came to the forefront of the world's media in an uncanny manner. Though miles away from newspaper offices and television studios, working in the gutters and filth, reporters sought her out and publicized her life and good works.

Mother Theresa was a symbol of love and compassion for all of us, and her death affected a great many people. At the time she died she was old and tired, her life force was weak and she needed to return to the spirit world.

Nevertheless, the timing of her death, just a few weeks after Princess Diana's death, was intended to focus the attention of the whole world; we lost two great humanitarians within days of each other. Her death was a reinforcement of the same message.

Now is the time for mankind to pay attention to the signs around and turn back to God.

Let brotherly love continue.
Be not forgetful to entertain strangers
for thereby some have
entertained Angels unaware.

– Hebrews 13:1-2

REINCARNATION
THE SOUL'S JOURNEY

*R*eincarnation means literally 'the eternal journey'. The journey our spirit makes as we live life after life, refining our soul's development and spiritual education. Self perfection is a slow process.

When we die and leave the world, as we know it, our life continues in a different form. Our eternal soul leaves the body behind and returns to our true home in the spiritual world. Our earthly death releases the soul and we occupy another dimension.

Once we enter heaven, we go through a life review. Individually, we each re-live our life in the presence of God. We have the opportunity to experience all of the love, joy, sorrow and pain we have ever caused. Not only do we re-experience the emotions from our point of view, but more importantly from the other person's perspective. Seeing all of the small hurts and smiles long forgotten. Feeling the big emotional scars and loving humanitarian acts we are personally responsible for. We take stock of our life on Earth. The lessons we have learned and what lessons we still need to accomplish. The debts we owe and what debts have been repaid. We review our life objectively with God, our Guardian Angels and Spirit Guides lovingly watching with sympathetic understanding. In heaven there is only love and truth, we stand bathed in God's radiant light knowing our shortcomings and our soul's attributes. We are our own judge, we are our harshest critic.

After the life review process we move into healing. It is a place where the soul rests and recuperates after the long difficult trials of a life on earth. The period of healing the soul is a type of purification, mending the emotional scars that have been inflicted.

Without the element of time in the spirit world, it is difficult to conceive a recognized period for the process, but after the healing of the soul there is freedom to do whatever pleases the soul. People tend to think we just float around in Heaven, but the reality is we are very active and productive. Our options are unlimited, some spirits teach, they garden, fish, are healers, and some are in training to become spirit guides. Earth was made as a reflection of Heaven, but Heaven is perfect. Whatever you can imagine, you have the ability to create there.

When we are completely refreshed, our soul gets ready, with the help of the Council and our guides, who monitor our soul's development, for another incarnation and revisit to earth. This process can take many decades or centuries, as we understand time on Earth. It is a slow process and a long journey.

Despite many translations of the Bible we can still see traces of reincarnation and karma that haven't been lost. In the book of Matthew there are two, Jesus was telling his disciples that John the Baptist was the reincarnation of Elias. "Elias has come already but they knew him not...then the disciples understood that he spoke of John the Baptist." The Jewish people were waiting for a sign that Elias had returned to Earth.

Before we reincarnate we choose the detail of our next life, our gender, mother and father, our life situations, family environment and the physical location where we will live. As in all things, we make our own choice of family to suit our needs for the development of our soul.

Whenever we face a situation, danger, or times of stress we should remember that the crisis is necessary for our spiritual development. Most people learn lessons the hard way, through difficulty there comes growth. There are no accidents, there are consequences for all of our actions; everything we do is in God's grand plan. So when issues arise, we should see them as stepping stones not as stumbling blocks.

Some people recall lives they have lived previously,

this is called 'past life memory'. They may recall people, places or events that are familiar from a previous existence. These thoughts and memories impinge on our daily consciousness as flashes of impressions. Déjà vu is often associated with past life memories. Dreams are another source by which we access our past lives.

A form of hypnosis called 'Past Life Regression' provides a platform which allows some people to access their past life memories hidden in their current subconscious mind. These regressions, when successful, can give fascinating and colorful insights into history and the subject's previous incarnations. Past Life Regression can be a great help in curing phobias and fears.

I strongly recall one of my past lives when I was a Native American medicine woman. I have many vivid memories of life on the Great Plains and living with my family in a tribe. My previous incarnation as a medicine woman and the knowledge gained then has passed with me into this life, those experiences assist me now when I diagnose potential areas of illness in people and advise them to seek medical attention.

There are many other examples of people who remember previous lives. Young children, who without any training can perform classical music scores, complete strangers who meet for the first time yet feel a great bonding and affinity with each other. Housewives who understand complex mathematical formulae, way beyond their educational level; all of these phenomena demonstrate that people can experience flashes of memory that open a window into their previous lives.

*   *   *

Sometimes a soul chooses to come into this life with a physical or mental handicap. This is a free will choice made by the soul specifically when there is a powerful purpose or when there are intense lessons to be learned.

Some souls that incarnate with a physical handicap are to repay a karmic debt; a form of severe payback for something they have done to another human in another, previous life. Before incarnating into an imperfect body they choose in spirit how they will repay their debt by living out a life of hardship in this life.

The decision made, the soul then looks for the appropriate family to join with. They seek a family that would benefit from the earthly hardships of having a handicapped member join their family.

The soul knows that each family member can have the opportunity for personal growth, depending on how they choose to interact with the handicapped family member.

There are others, such as autistic and Downs Syndrome children, who are highly evolved souls. They come to earth in handicapped bodies for a much greater purpose. They have chosen to lessen the world's karmic debt, they are paying a price in this life for the whole of mankind. Just as Jesus did when he died on the cross. "Victim Soul" is a term used to describe some of these loving souls.

There are hundreds of examples, some well recorded, of special children who despite overwhelming physical handicaps still astound their families and others with their profound knowledge of life.

There is a boy in Texas who has never been able to walk or talk, his feeble limbs have little muscle tone and his eyes are slightly crossed. To many people it might appear 'no one is home' when they first see him. He sits and stares vacantly most of the time.

From birth he has been an important part of his family. Following a normal birth and early months he stopped developing at nineteen months old. Doctors could not understand his failure to thrive.

Undeterred by his severe physical and mental handicaps his mother continued to love and cherish her son. She was determined to communicate with him, constantly reading and talking with him. She even made an alphabet board to spell words to him.

Blessed with strong faith, the family continued the one sided communications. Three years later, the boy started to spell sentences back to his family. The words he spelled out were not the ordinary thoughts of a young child.

His writings were about a beautiful glorious God. Today he continues his dialog about Heaven and God's infinite goodness. His works have now been compiled into a book. The boy's words and essays paint a picture of a highly evolved soul, a spiritual mind far removed from the physical constraints and shackles of a handicapped child living in Texas.

How many others are there in the world? How many have never had a persistent parent? How many children and adults have been given life sentences and cast aside, discarded and simply labeled mentally disabled?

There are many wise souls living spiritual lives in other dimensions. They respond to love, we must cherish and nurture these souls and we must never judge another souls chosen path.

Every time we come into contact with a disabled person it is a test. Will we be rude or unkind, or are we willing to help those that seem less fortunate than us?

Our karma will carry the mark of our interaction with those less fortunate than ourselves, for all of time. The simple rule should be 'Never judge a book by it's cover'.

We reincarnate to accomplish our given missions, learn, and help satisfy our karmic obligations and to fulfill our contracts with different individuals that we made in the spirit world.

Souls group together as a spiritual family and we often incarnate with others from our spiritual clan who are on the same level of development. Because of the close bond in the many lifetimes spent together on earth we have to continue working out karmic issues and individual contracts throughout many subsequent lives.

Two souls often contract with each other to work on a specific issue during one lifetime such as love, forgiveness, betrayal, lust or greed. Once the soul has worked through the issue then the karmic debt is paid and the soul can move on to another part of the educational process.

Soulmates are souls that have experienced many loving incarnations together and have a very deep bond that goes beyond this one lifetime they experience together.

Because we have incarnated through eons of time we have more than one soulmate, we have developed close bonds and loving relationships with several souls.

Life on earth is one of the most difficult planets on which we incarnate because of the duality that exists here. Good and bad, love and fear, male and female, light and dark are all examples of the issues that make life so difficult here.

I have a tremendous example of reincarnation, regression and karma that I would like to share:

A spiritually minded woman came to me for a past life reading, she knew her relationship with her husband was not only about this life time but there was a soul connection to past life experiences.

Living a difficult life she was interested enough to save her marriage. She wanted to look into the past to see what the lessons and teachings were to help her today.

During my prayer and meditation I saw very clearly that she and her husband were soul mates. In the spiritual realm their love and respect for each other was grand!

As I started the reading Sheila told me that they had been married for ten years.

Scott, her husband, was a hard worker providing a beautiful home and luxury cars. But emotionally he was distant, very deep and complex.

He had a dictatorial personality and wanted to control every situation. Emotionally unavailable he was non-supportive and verbally abusive, even to their two beautiful children. He chose not to be affectionate or participate in their lives.

Sheila, my client, was the family's foundation. She was a business owner, running a business and the family meant she had two full time jobs. After ten years of a one sided marriage, she had had enough.

As I asked 'The Counsel' in the spirit world to show me their past life incarnations, the doorways began to open, revealing a unique vista.

I saw an ancient Roman city. Scott was a wealthy man in his 40's with a large household and many slaves to do his bidding.

Sheila was one of them, actually one of his favorites. In that life he was cruel to her even though he cared about her. She worked hard to please him, but nothing was ever good enough. She had been given more freedom than the other slaves and soon planned her escape.

Three more lifetimes I saw, all with the same theme. Scott being the unemotional lover in each life, continually mistreating Sheila until she'd had her fill and would leave him. In present day the pattern was re-playing itself again.

I explained what I had seen to Sheila and asked if she could see the lesson they had agreed to in spirit. She answered quietly, "Yes, he is teaching me the lesson of forgiveness. Each life time the great love I've had for him has turned into hate."

The lesson of forgiveness is the most divine teaching; it is the one of the hardest lessons we have to learn on Earth. Often it may seem someone is going out of his or her way to deliberately hurt us. The repetition of these wounds can fester into hate, bitterness and even tragic violence.

In reality we have chosen this lesson in spirit. In Sheila's case she asked her best friend in spirit to help her learn the lesson of forgiveness. Now she has awakened from the painful illusions and realized she can finally accomplish her lesson.

Sheila has moved on with her life. She has forgiven her husband of all of his cruelties. She has had several long talks with Scott, no longer pointing the blame at him but explaining she has grown past their relationship. It's her time to spread her wings and fly.

Sheila and Scott are now divorced. She has blessed him and moved forward with her life. Scott is not spiritually awake in this lifetime. He still occasionally tries to create drama and push Sheila's buttons, but she greets his maneuvering and attacks with loving actions.

At the end of their lives, when they once again meet in spirit, there will be a great celebration between the two soul mates.

Earthly relationships are not always to be long term. We learn our lessons and move on. We do not have to continue to suffer and go on with the drama. I think that in this case, five lifetimes have been enough.

*   *   *

Many clients ask me how I can access past lives.

Some people on Earth have been granted a look at "The Book of Life", sometimes called the Akashic Records. Man records each of his lifetimes, so there is a document of his soul's journey, right down to the tiniest detail. Every thought, action and word that soul's incarnation has ever spoken is recorded.

This is a permanent record, reviewed every time a soul chooses it's next incarnation. The record lists the already learned lessons so the soul can understand which spiritual lessons still need to be mastered and which environment will enhance those lessons.

When I am looking at a client's past life I see the activity of that soul's journey in their aura. I can see where issues stem from, where past life wounds still affect a client's present life and the Karmic relationships with family members.

Similarly, I see imprints we carry on our soul, of past

life events. That's why we have unexplainable likes and dislikes, those choices are imprinted on our essence; so some people are frightened of water for no apparent reason, some are frightened of flying and some have an irrational fear of fire.

Old Souls

All souls were created at the same time. Some souls choose to incarnate more often, really applying themselves to learn spiritual lessons. Those souls termed 'old souls' have set high standards for themselves in the spirit world.

So when they return to earth, they arrive ready to work through the challenges they have set up for themselves in spirit.

The term 'old souls' does not necessarily reflect the number of incarnations they have endured, but rather the amount of soul experiences gathered and learned from. That is what determines whether we are an old or young soul.

When a soul has completed his or her development on earth it no longer needs earthly incarnations. Perfecting the soul is not likely, until at least sixty incarnations have been experienced. These are the exceptional souls. Most of my readings have shown me souls incarnate hundreds of times.

The planet Earth is a big schoolhouse where souls learn important spiritual truths or lessons. The difficulty of life here means that the lessons are so much harder to learn, and positive results here are harder to achieve. Each soul takes a risk when choosing to come here. We risk creating more Karmic debt by forgetting who we truly are, "perfect children of God". Those that incarnate on Earth are greatly celebrated in the spirit world.

*See I am sending an Angel
ahead of you
to guard you along the way
and to bring you to
the place I have prepared.*

– Exodus 23:20

CHAPTER

8

WE ALL HAVE FREE WILL

*F*ree will is a gift that has been bestowed upon us by our creator, God. God's will is our will. God experiences earthly life through us.

Society has imposed laws that condition our lives, but inside or outside those constraints we each make many choices, and almost daily we make choices that we consider good or bad. Sometimes the choice is an easy call, but sometimes tempted by greed, lust, envy or another dark motive, we use our free will to consciously make a poor choice. Often we seem to 'get away' with those poor choices, we reap the benefits of cheating and gain advantage over others without any penalty being imposed on us. We feel that we've won a victory. But be sure for every action, there is a consequence.

Know that God does not judge us. When we make the better choice in life we are happier and fulfilled. In God's eyes there is no 'right' or 'wrong', just experiences to learn from.

When we use our free will to make a better choice

and do a good deed, help someone in need, or give selflessly without thought of reward or benefit from others, sometimes such good deeds go unnoticed. We certainly don't feel to have benefited in an earthbound way, but we may derive a certain feeling of satisfaction or pleasure from helping somebody less fortunate than ourselves. That feeling is the warm glow of goodness and love that always fills our soul, when we do good, a little love overflows and we feel an uplifting in our hearts. Remember that these good deeds are also re-lived during our soul's life review.

Free will is a great gift that enables us to choose what we want or how we want our life to be. Some think of it as a curse, for at times it may appear as such to those who don't understand the benefits of having a free will.

It is our birthright, from the day we are born through the time of death, we are able to choose our own destiny. At the moment of death, we still have the choice where we will go. This choice in the afterlife is somewhat based upon our personal belief system.

Free will comes with a huge responsibility. For every choice we make there is a consequence. When man thinks about free will, he thinks of it as meaning the potential to do things that are the opposite of Gods will. But actually our free will gives us unlimited potential to create a perfect world. God has given us all of the resources to create a utopian life, paradise on Earth. By making the better choices we can then truly create our happiness.

We must keep in mind that choices we make not only affect ourselves but impact others as well. Many times we are not even aware of how our actions or words have impacted others. The choices we make can often create a domino effect or a rippling impression that can continue to be felt, either positive or negative.

The whole purpose of free will is to learn from our experiences, to come into an awareness and a greater understanding of how making the better choice improves our whole environment.

We gain wisdom and understanding through many incarnations and the choices that we have made. We frequently make the same choices over and over again. Sometimes it takes several lifetimes to learn from a negative choice. We keep making the same mistake until we learn that it is not the best choice. A soul's growth or evolution takes place when the soul learns the lesson. We learn these lessons at our own pace.

We are here to experience all aspects of life. To learn the lessons of loving unconditionally, compassion for others, forgiveness, and self love.

Once we have learned our spiritual lessons we no

longer need to return to this planet because we have gleaned all of the knowledge we can from this reality that is based on duality. This is how we evolve to a higher consciousness.

The whole purpose God allows us to choose our experiences is for us to choose to return to God of our own free will. Not because we are forced, but because we want to be part of God, to come back to his perfection. We are to return to our own true divine self, the perfect part of us that is within us, waiting for us to recognize our divinity, our inner light of God.

Through free will and being able to choose our own path we will find peace and balance. Most of all, it is a journey that each soul makes to regain perfection while in human form.

Angels don't have free will as humans do, for they already represent perfection and can never change their state. Mankind is a blessed race of God's children for his greatest attribute is that he is able to grow and evolve, able to become one with God.

God's gift to man is an individual soul that may choose to become one with him. Man has hopes and desires. God intends humankind to be free, even if he uses his free will to defy God's laws.

When we return to the spirit world we have our life review which is an evaluation of the life we just experienced. Our deeds and actions are all reviewed to see what was learned and what we still need to improve upon. During the life review we re-examine our relationships with others. We can then see those we helped and those we hurt. In that way we can see how our free will has been imposed on others.

Leaders through the centuries have demonstrated how their free will had profound effects on the mass population. Not only affected mankind in their life time but continue to influence and color humanity.

Imagine Hitler during his life review. At that time he had to experience and literally feel all the pain, sorrow and torture he was responsible for.

In our life review we experience every thing we have said, done, and thought. We experience it from our perspective as well from the other person's point of view. We re-live and re-experience these events and words as the other person, and so we feel the impact of our free will, just as the other person felt it.

Hitler's free will affected many more people than he was aware of. Only at the time of his death and subsequent life review did he know the complete impression he had left on humanity.

He then understood the complete negative impression he left on the world. It was like a ripple effect that continues to affect mankind. Today the Jewish culture still feels the pain and the sorrow, and many Europeans continue to feel guilt from Hitler's rule.

One man made such a drastic impact on millions of souls. One person's free will can and does affect the mass consciousness.

Jesus demonstrated a positive example of free will. He touched many souls during his short incarnation here on Earth as a master teacher to mankind. He taught by example how free will not only affects us, but the lives of others.

One soul changed the consciousness of millions and to this day his teachings of love still have a profound affect on millions. Jesus changed the mass population in a positive way by demonstrating and living his life from unconditional love.

There is a difference between having free will while we are in the spirit world and the free will we experience while on Earth. In the spirit world we have a great wealth of knowledge that we do not have access to when we are in human form working from our lower consciousness.

Our consciousness, which is our ego, subconscious, intellect, or lower mind is the state of consciousness that most humans work from while on Earth. The 'Higher Self' is the part of us that remembers our true self; the part of us that is connected to God and is in tune with all knowledge.

When we return to our true state of being, we are without ego and we know only love and truth. In the spirit world we have clarity and insight to the solutions we are seeking. We will automatically make the correct choice that is for our best and highest good. In human form our decision making process is clouded with ego. The veil or curtain between this world and the heavens does not allow us to remember everything consciously.

We come into our life on Earth with an agenda and karma that will play itself out. That is why we do not have full access to our whole spiritual self and the knowledge we possess. The whole point in coming to this earthly plane is to grow and evolve to a higher state of spiritual consciousness.

KARMA - REAPING WHAT WE SOW

*K*arma is God's Universal Law, simply put it is the immutable law of cause and effect.

Every time we make a choice, right or wrong, good or bad, conscious or unconscious we affect the balance of life and nature, we affect our Karma. Whatever we feel, say, think or do creates a consequence that will come back to us at some future time.

When we make a positive choice then that choice will come back tenfold to affect our life. Similarly, when we make a negative choice then that too will come back to us tenfold.

I explain to my students an analogy that describes Karma as being a type of celestial debit card filled with free choices and potential actions, for us to spend as we see fit. We use our free will and spend from our debit card as we wish, but one day the consequences of those choices will come back to us.

Every action, choice, or thought we make during our tenure on Earth is recorded on our soul and when we leave this life we carry that record with us.

Everything we've ever done and thought throughout this life, previous lives and in lives yet to come is written in the Book of Life, sometimes called the 'Akashic Records' or 'Hall of Records'. This Library keeps a permanent account of our karma.

Highly evolved spiritualists know that the Hall of Records is managed and maintained in the heavens by a select group of twelve Ascended Masters that are called 'The Council' or 'The Elders'.

The Council maintains the Book of Life, they oversee karma for all of humanity, both for individuals and for groups of people that have created group karma, such as those involved in the Holocaust, or those involved in black slavery.

Events that happen to us in this life can be a result of karma payback from choices we made earlier in life or the result of actions we took in former lives.

However the law of karma is not a one-time experience that only applies in this life, we can feel the effects of karma in this life today as we pay the consequences of our actions from previous reincarnations.

The effects of karma can be plain to see:

There are people who seem to lead a charmed life, content with their lot, with loving partners and caring children. They could be benefiting from a positive karmic payback from a previous life.

Whereas, some people are loners, malcontents or even evil, they never prosper and fail at their every enterprise. They could be feeling the negative karmic effects from their previous choices in a former life.

What is the purpose of karma?

God wants us all to be essentially good and loving. He created the law of karma to ensure the balance of positive and negative on the earth. Karma can be viewed as a tool combined with an incentive to help us make the better choices in life. The laws of karma are repeated eternally until we realize that we should make the better choices either in this life or in a later life, for only then can our souls evolve to another, higher plane.

There are different types of karma that we work through as individuals and in groups of people.

Individual karma is lessons that each soul is personally responsible to work out in our own way and at our own pace. We are eternal, we have all the time in the world, and then some. Each soul has personal lessons to learn, teachings to give, and missions to fulfill. Each soul has a purpose and a grand plan. That is what makes life so interesting.

Group karma is a lesson that a large group of souls

inflicts upon another group of people. Group karma is experienced as prejudice, whether racial, religious, economical, or intellectual. It is experienced as a deliberate separation of one group who thinks they are superior to another group of people. The dominant group that chooses to do injustices to another must repay the karmic debt. In this life or another lifetime they must personally experience the specific prejudice they chose to impose on others.

Instant Karma is a lesson that comes back to us immediately, we experience the effects right away. Like when a person goes out of their way to say hurtful words to anyone. Then within a very short time someone unexpectedly says something unkind to him or her. That is a small example of how instant karma comes right back to us. What we have done to another has come to us so we can take another look at our actions and learn from them.

Physical karma is a harsh debt that must be repaid by experiencing a physical deformity, an illness, or a mental disorder. They are health issues caused by misdeeds from this lifetime or more frequently from a past life.

A client of mine was suffering from severe female problems and the doctors were not able to help her. Their recommendation was the removal her female organs. This was not a solution that she was comfortable with and chose instead to seek other advice.

During a private reading, the information that her Guardian Angels gave me was that this physical problem stemmed from a previous life and some childhood trauma. As I looked into the Akashic Records I saw one of her previous lives.

Her soul had incarnated as a man in ancient times, I could see she was a Viking soldier of some kind, armed with a sword. In that cruel historic time, I clearly saw him during an attack on a defenseless village. He pulled a woman from a rough shack and raped her before fatally stabbing her in the abdomen.

Following the rules of karma, in this life she had incarnated as a woman and was now suffering the karmic payback, as she endured ongoing pain and distress caused by her malfunctioning female reproductive organs.

Mental karma is a lesson about verbal abuse. It is a payback from mocking, making fun of, or be-littling a person intentionally. It is psychological damage that has been done purposefully with words.

Emotional damage to others is just as powerful as physical damage. People do not understand how deeply they can wound another with a razor sharp tongue. We can change a person's life with just a sentence.

We must take responsibility for our words for they have great power. Choose your words carefully because you cannot take them back.

Suspended karma is a debt that has not been forgotten, but only postponed. The right opportunity must present itself so the lesson can play itself out. The time, the person, and the place all affect the way the lessons are played out. Sometimes it may be several lifetimes before the perfect opportunity arises again.

Most karma can be worked through in the lifetime it is brought to our attention. Once karma is recognized and worked on, it is resolved. We will not have to repeat the lesson because we have learned from the experiences.

When younger, less experienced souls born onto this planet understand that the law of karma follows us throughout our lives and into the next then there will be a great change throughout mankind.

Older souls that have learned and remembered the lessons of karma from many former reincarnations evolve to a new level. Once they have graduated to such a plane that they fulfilled their karmic debt they no longer need to incarnate on the earth plane.

Knowledge of the law of karma gives us the power to learn from our mistakes.

All the arrangements that are
carried out between
Heaven and Earth are
carried out through Angels.

– The Essence of Islam

She Talks with Angels

CHAPTER

10

GUARDIAN ANGELS AND ANGELIC REALMS

*A*ngels are God's helpers and messengers, a group of entities created to do God's bidding. They come from unconditional love and are a part of God's essence.

All angels are created equal by God, although there is a hierarchy or ranking amongst them. Archangels are the highest ranking angels, closest to God, each of them has a specific task, and they in turn have legions of helpers to assist them.

Earth angels, including fairies, cherubs and mermaids are lower ranked angels who perform tasks for humanity and the Mother Earth. Of all the different ranks of angels, we are most familiar with the earth angels. Throughout history, earth angels have manifested themselves in a physical form, so confirming the existence of the celestial realm to man.

Paintings, statues and writing confirm their frequent appearances throughout the ages. These angels are an integral part of modern folklore and their continued acceptance today is demonstrated by the number of parents who teach their young about their Guardian Angels and the fairies in the garden.

Archangels

Archangels work with many people from a distance. These powerful Angels respond to prayers when people call upon them for help with a specific task. Each Archangel has specific areas of responsibilities, areas they personally oversee and govern, whereas our Guardian Angels are with us at all times. Archangels pop into our lives when called on or when needed, but our Guardian Angels are assigned to assist us full time during our life span.

Archangels reside in the seven levels of heaven. Each Archangel is the ruler of one of the levels in heaven.

Archangel Michael is the right hand of God, and the Light Warrior Angel who leads the celestial army. He protects all humanity, not only our physical bodies but also our souls from danger, darkness and threats.

He commands legions of angels who do his bidding here on earth. He sends angels to help souls in need and helps us protect our eternal being from damage and darkness.

I personally work with the Archangel Michael. He is with me, personally protecting my physical body and my soul from attacks. He protects me full time, rather like a Guardian Angel. Lightworkers like myself that have been chosen to be a messenger of God often attract more negative attention than normal people. Working in the public eye, doing God's work, I need the added protection of an Archangel.

My mission here on Earth is to make a great impact with the messages from the spirit world. I have been told by Michael that the time is now to reach the larger population, that God and his angels are helping me to quickly move into earthly recognition by using the media, speaking events, televisions shows, and books to spread their message.

Michael works with me because I am also a spiritual warrior sent to earth by God to give his message to the masses. I am considered part of his family. When most people call on Michael to ask for his assistance they receive his help through one of his many Angel helpers. When I call upon him, I always get Michael himself. I am blessed and grateful for this assistance.

I need the great protection of a warrior Angel while clearing negative spirits from places and especially when performing exorcisms on children. My spiritual power is magnified many times when I call upon Michael for help.

I could not remove dangerous supernatural entities from a human without great faith and his assistance.

Archangel Raphael is the Angel appointed by God to be in charge of all healing. His responsibilities include healing our body and soul and overseeing healers of all types, such as shamans, doctors and nurses. Raphael is also responsible for healing the Earth.

Raphael works with me when doing healing work. I call upon him to help heal emotional problems and physical illness. I am considered a healer. During my readings clients who sit in front of me often receive a healing. I call upon Raphael at the beginning of my reading and he or one of his Angels assists me. Each person that comes to see me needs to be healed on some level, whether it be emotional wounds, physical weakness or illness.

During the course of a spiritual reading, clients receive a specific healing that they need on a cellular level. I don't even need to touch them for Raphael's power is great; he is an instrument in healing through God.

When a healing occurs, it is greatly based on the person's faith. There is no specific process or length of time for healing. If the person has strong faith then the healing can be immediate. All you need is strong faith in God and the desire to be healed. Healing can be instantaneous; what most people would consider an immediate miracle.

Archangel Gabriel is a messenger and the Angel of Communication. He brings very important messages from God to the physical world, often being called the Voice of God. Gabriel appeared to Mary, the Blessed Mother, and told her that she was chosen to be the mother of the Son of God.

Gabriel helps me to convey spiritual truths to the public and to the media. I am considered a truth speaker. People are shocked at my honesty, and sometimes that honesty can seem blunt. I relay the messages from the spirit world without editing or candy coating them. Gabriel told me a long time ago I must always say what ever is given to me from the spirit world no matter how outlandish the message might seem.

Over the years, I have evolved and now benefit from an increase in my psychic abilities, now I have the gift of prophecy. Gabriel has told me to get ready to share my visions of the future with the masses.

Archangel Uriel is the Angel of Light, God's essence and the eternal fire within. Uriel is the Angel of inspiration and God's wisdom. He teaches us the path to understanding God.

Uriel works through me as inspiration. My drive to do God's work by relaying spiritual truths received from the heavens consumes my daily life. My mission in life is to inspire others to seek truth and a higher understanding of God's love and greatness. Uriel helps me to connect to the source of all spiritual knowledge and ancient truths that mankind has forgotten through the ages. My great love of God and my love for humanity are my motivation to be in the service of others. For without love and devotion to spirit, all spiritual study remains just an intellectual pursuit.

Fallen Angels

Lucifer was once an archangel that was the closest to God. The name Lucifer means "light of God or The bringer of the Light." He was God's favorite. Lucifer had a desire to experience life much like humans do. He wanted to know what it was like to have free will and choice, to be a co-creator of life. He felt that humans were a wonderful race that God created. They could experience a wide range of emotions and desires: joy, sadness, pleasure, pain, wealth, poverty and power. Humans have the ability to grow and evolve, to work through earthly experiences toward the ultimate experience of perfection and returning to God. To join with God and become one with the source.

Lucifer and the other heavenly Angels were a race

that God made to represent purity of spirit and unconditional love. In Angels these characteristics are unchangeable, they only know unconditional love.

As Lucifer looked down upon the earth with curiosity and envy, he saw all the options and vast experiences mankind could choose. They had so many choices available to them, good and bad. They had the ability to choose to co-create whatever they desired. This was very appealing to Lucifer.

God understood this is what Lucifer wanted. So God in his great love for his favorite, granted Lucifer the opportunity to experience life. God told Lucifer that when he left the heavens he would forget the privileged knowledge of Heaven.

Hearing this Lucifer did not want to go alone. He asked the other Angels to go with him. At that moment there was a division in Heaven. God allowed Lucifer and his legions of Angels to enter the lower astral realms and the Earth plane. Traditional religion would have us believe that these angels were thrown out of Heaven. This is untrue. God allowed his beloved Angels to leave Heaven, and they were eager to explore.

There was a large price to pay for this journey. As Lucifer and his Angels descended to Earth they went through "The Veil" and forgot their way home. The Veil or sometimes it is called a curtain is the division between Heaven and Earth. It hides the truth from us all and it does not allow Lucifer to see his heavenly home or who he once was. As the Angels descended to earth they came into a state of amnesia. They no longer possessed the recollection of Heaven, all heavenly knowledge or the remembrance of the light of God that resides within us all.

Just as the human soul goes through this veil each time we incarnate. We also experience the temporary loss of our detailed memory of our glorious home in Heaven until we return again to the spirit realm and full memory is restored.

This was a great surprise to Lucifer and his Angels as they descended to Earth. He and his Angels are lost without their memory. They have become disenchanted with Earth, the lower Astral Realms, and their plans to create. They want to return to heaven but they have lost their way. They want to return to the grandeur of God and his infinite source of Love and Light.

Angels

God created Angels to help him in his ongoing work, there are literally billions of angels in the spirit world.

Angels are not concerned with gender or physical appearances. They exhibit and radiate bright light and total unconditional love. Angel's bright light has been traditionally depicted in artwork as a gleaming halo, but in reality the entire Angel glows with God's love.

Guardian Angels

God appoints at least two Guardian Angels to help each of us from the exact moment our soul enters a body and we are born into this world. These angels are with us from birth, through all our life and are waiting for us at the moment of our physical death. After death they help our soul make the transition into the realm of Heaven.

Our Guardian Angels help and protect us throughout our life, they are our support team, always ready and always with us. God gives us angel helpers to make it easier and safer for our souls as we work through our life on earth. They are God's messengers, offering unconditional love - God's love.

We can make contact with our angels by prayer, dreams and meditation. They are waiting, but it's up to us to acknowledge them and open the door and let them into our lives. Angels cannot interfere with our free will and choice, they wait patiently for us to invite them into our lives but won't ever force themselves upon us.

When we do invite them into our lives through the

power of prayer they respond and help us with our earthly problems.

We can ask them to give us a sign that they have heard our prayers and our angels or spirit guides will provide us with a recognizable confirmation.

People have different experiences after praying for a confirmation. The signs are subtle, perhaps a fragrance, a feeling of being watched, a glimpse of a figure out the corner of the eye, a knocking or the sound of music, angels don't want to scare us with their presence and so they take a low key, quiet approach.

Angels can manifest themselves and appear before us, visiting in many different ways, such as taking human form to warn of us of impending danger or to test our humanity to others. Angels can also appear at times of great emotional upheaval or just before we die.

I feel blessed that I know my own angels, I know their names and what they look like and I seek their assistance regularly. I consider my angels as my best personal friends. When they manifest before me it is a magnificent experience.

I met with my guardian angels following a serious car crash. I was badly injured and lay near to death, when I left my body and moved into the spirit world my guardian angels were waiting for me. They told me that it was not yet time for me to die and returned me to my physical body.

Since then, one of my angels manifested to me when I prayed and requested a confirmation of her presence. She assured me that my angels were there and with me at all times.

Once I awoke to a beautiful blonde Angel, she had vivid purple eyes and large white wings. Her aura was so brilliant it made my room glow. Her presence was made to me as a personal confirmation of her daily presence and her overwhelming love for me. I feel I am very blessed when they manifest in physical form on my behalf. It is a gift from the spirit world and I am truly grateful.

At other times I have heard heavenly music, Angels have appeared as balls of light, and at times they call out my name. Angels communicate with me through telepathy and emotions. They speak to me intuitively or through feelings that wash over me so I understand the emotion they are trying to convey to me.

Guardian Angels are our guides, they do not shape our destiny, we alone are responsible for things and events that happen to us during our life, but they can create opportunities and encourage us at various times in our lives. Our angels are a direct link into the spirit world and protect us from dangers and evil, inspire us and guide us along the path of life.

Earth Angels

Earth Angels or Nature Spirits live in a place called the fairy realm. As in most folklore handed down through the generations of life there is an essential truth in folklore about fairies and the fairy kingdoms. Fables and stories of humans interacting with fairies were once known as fact.

Today these nature spirits still work with humanity, but they are rarely seen. They live in the next astral plane or dimension of the spirit world. Anytime humans interact with spirits from other planes of existence there is a general disbelief or fear in the population.

Through the ages we have turned our backs on our intuitive nature and so we created, and still continue, a trend of ignoring other planes of existence. Very young children and animals still see into the fairy realm with ease for their minds are open and unprejudiced.

For adults, once shifting consciousness was as easy as opening a door, but time and lack of use have taken away that skill and nowadays it takes deliberate effort.

With effort and belief in the fairy realm you will soon start to sense it and if you are of good heart you may even get a glimpse of that other plane!

Earth Angels are a category of God's angels that are

divided into the four elemental forces. They are the Fire, Air, Earth, and Water Spirits.

These nature spirits are more than just elementals, like humans and animals they have distinct personalities. Each of the four families are purposeful beings with feelings, talents and they react to how nature is being treated. They are nature, they are the essence of Mother Earth. They are her soul.

Their personalities are as individual as humankind, some are loving, kind and helpful, others are funny pranksters, mischievous borrowers, or angry little deities. Their actions and reactions are formed depending on how they and their environments are being treated.

Within each of the four elemental families there are many types of races of beings, and each elemental has a hierarchy or ranking according to their position and size. The larger the fairy the higher in rank it is. Each element has a King or Queen that reports to the Archangel over its element. Each elemental family has an important function for the wellbeing of humanity. Without these other realm helpers, humanity would fail to thrive. They are our brothers and sisters; our family.

Gnomes - Earth Nature Spirits

The elemental spirits of the Earth come in all shapes sizes and colors, Gnomes, Trolls, Knockers, Brownies, Leprechauns, Divas, Pixies and Little People just to name a few. Elves and dwarves are generic terms used for Gnomes without wings.

Most elementals live in the ground, but some of the darker colored elves prefer taking up residence in dark places around the home, like attics, basements or closets.

These good-natured elves and brownies especially love children and animals. They will adopt a home for the joy of offering help and support.

Leprechauns protect buried treasure and help to protect animals in their vicinity.

Entryways into their dimension are water wells, holes in the ground, hollow trees and fairy mounds. Each entry point has its own protector or guardian spirit.

Gnomes are the elementals in charge of the soil, they are living essence of the earth. They are the actual souls of the soil, rocks and plants. They create minerals and promote the richness of the soil and work to produce healthy growing plants, trees, and crops.

Gnomes and elves work hard to maintain Earth's physical structure and its eco-balance.

Divas are the little spirits that are the life of each plant and flower on earth. They are responsible for adding beautiful colors to our world as well as with producing food to sustain us.

Trees have many spirits that work together to maintain its long lifespan. Tree spirits are as large as the tree itself. We can imagine how large the spirit of a California Redwood must be!

Many people are afraid to walk alone in the woods at night for they get the eerie feeling of being watched. The tree spirits are watching as the people pass by.

Trees have many helpers, the elves that live in the branches, the gnomes turning the soil around the root system and even the little divas that promote the blooms and fruit of the tree.

Each forest has its own lady of the forest who oversees the welfare of her specific forest. She is one of the largest Earth Angels. She takes on a human like form and reports to the king of the Earth Elemental spirits. The Gnomes and the fairies are governed by their king and protected by and answer to Archangel Uriel.

The Earth Elements teach us to understand the hidden forces of nature and provide us with trees, food for us to eat and a colorful place for us to grow and evolve.

Nymphs - Water Nature Spirits

Water covers two thirds of the planet Earth and humans contain a large proportion of water in our physical make up. The Water world is a whole world within itself. There are many types of water Nymphs, Undines, Lorelei, Bogs, Mermaids, and Mermen who inhabit this water world.

Wherever there is water activity, rain, ponds, lakes, rivers, puddles and oceans there are Water Nymphs at work. They can be as small as a drop of water or as large as the entire water source.

Water provides the most traveled route into the fairy realm. The most magical points of entry are any place where water meets land, such as, islands, beaches, waterfalls or any intersecting waterway.

The fairy kingdoms that exist beneath the sea or a lake are hidden by the reflection of the water's surface.

The Water Fairies or Sea Sprites are small and semi-transparent to our eyes. They are seen in the ocean waves riding in bubbles or on sea animals such as seahorses or turtles.

Mermaids and Mermen are next to the largest in size. They have the ability to shape shift into dolphins or seals when they want to be in close proximity to humans. The Sea Sprites are very curious about mankind. Water Nymphs connect with us through our dreams and our emotions. They help awaken our creativeness. Water represents spirituality.

Water Nymphs work to cleanse our water sources and so promote the health of sea life. Humanity could not survive and exist without their help. They answer to the King of the Sea, Neptune who in turn answers to Archangel Gabriel.

Sylphs - Air Spirits

The spirits of the air are called Sylphs. These spirits of the air have much more freedom than any other element for they are everywhere around us.

We see them as cloud formations, storms, wind and even breath. Through our breath we gain physical and mental power. The air spirits teach us to breathe deeply in meditation so that we can more easily attune ourselves to God. When they manifest Sylphs look transparent and wispy.

These lofty beings range from tiny to the giant storm fairies that bring major change to the Earth. The air spirits will sometimes take form and sit on the clouds, seen at times by airline passengers as they look out their windows.

Clouds form into shapes for communication with

us, they act as signs and pictures as messages. The air spirits encourage our telepathic abilities, intuitiveness and clairvoyance. Air is the tool that transports our thoughts and our intent. The air spirits make it possible for music to travel and our words. We use language to communicate with others and even the animals. They inspire our mental abilities and communicate with us through thought. The wind has its own voice that communicates with those who are sensitive enough to hear what it is saying.

These nature spirits control the weather and the Earth's atmosphere. They protect us from comets and asteroids and even from the damaged ozone layer that is caused by humanity.

Wind is the force of the Sylphs that can remove negativity. The storm fairies clear areas that are heavy with negativity including towns, buildings, people and plants. This allows new growth, a fresh start.

The air fairies are mischievous, with the power to move ships and airplanes off their courses. The Sylph is also a friend to humans; they love to be of service to us. They have saved many people lost and drifting at sea by pushing them towards safety.

At times, a Sylph will shapeshift into the form of an animal, always choosing a winged creature: swans, birds, butterflies, and eagles. They do this so they can connect to the humans they are so curious about. They will make their presence known to us by fragrance, feathers or sudden breezes.

The queen of the Sylphs reports to Archangel Raphael. Air is what divides heaven and earth!

Salamanders - The Fire Nature Spirits

The fire spirits are called the Salamanders. These are not to be confused with the four-legged amphibians. Of all the nature spirits, Salamanders are the hardest to understand and connect with. They are the most intelligent of all the Earth Angels and have the least interest in humans. Other Nature spirits are nurturing and loving to mankind, but this is not true of Salamanders.

Fire is always regarded as something mysterious and dangerous. The fire Salamanders include smoke fairies, Jinn or Genies, volcanic salamanders, lightning snakes and sun fairies.

Everywhere there is fire these spirits are present whether it be the soft gentle flame of candlelight or the roaring rapacious destruction of a forest fire. These hard to see nature spirits show themselves as the flicker of the flame, a puff of smoke, or a lightning bolt sometimes. They sometimes shapeshift into the form of a dragonfly, snake, or a firefly in order to spy on a human. They are unpredictable and hard to control.

Fire spirits use their energy as a clearing agent to rejuvenate and bring new life. They have the power of creation and destruction and move swiftly to clear negativity. They report to Archangel Michael, the warrior.

These nature spirits govern energy, warmth, and light. They are connected to our Inner Light. They help us master our kundalini energy and awaken our spiritual creativity.

*   *   *

There are many souls that God has created on the physical plane as well as in the spirit world. Every soul has a grand purpose.

The Earth Angels sustain our physical lives working with us in unison never asking for anything in return. The Water Spirits provide us with clean water to drink, water to cleanse and refresh our bodies. The Gnomes give us rejuvenated soil, healthy crops, and a place to build our homes. The spirits of the air give us fresh air to breathe and protect the atmosphere. The Fire Fairy cleanses the ground so renewal and rebirth may take place.

Without the help of these fairies, humans could not survive. They are Mother Natures' children, just as we are.

My hope is that these words have stirred your heart and you will open yourself up to the endless possibilities and the goodness of our universe. We humans are multi-dimensional beings with the capacity to perceive many of God's creations. We only have to open our minds, look around us and we can see God's magical creations everywhere.

CHAPTER

11

SPIRIT GUIDES AND SPIRITS

Spirits

A spirit or soul is our energy and the pure essence of each of us. It is our God-part-self, the part of us that is eternal and divine.

When we die our spirit leaves the body and can choose to move through the light into the spirit world.

There the spirit undergoes a 'life review', a process of self examination where all the actions, thoughts, feelings and emotions of the earthly life are reviewed; it is not a judgmental process, but rather a chance for evaluation of the soul's journey.

The spirit reviews its life on earth and gathers experience, learning from mistakes and evolving to a higher understanding of what purpose each experience has served.

The spirit retains human memories and the mind and personality of the human it once was, even though it has been elevated and resides in the celestial realm of heaven.

Life is a traumatic and tiring process and each soul needs time and space to recover from the trials of life on Earth. They heal and rest replenishing energy forces and undergo further learning. As eternal beings we constantly continue to learn and evolve in the spirit world.

After the healing process is complete, a soul can then check in on their earthly families. It's not unusual for a soul just leaving a body behind to be greeted by family members and loved ones that have died previously. They are easily recognizable for many spirits retain the same physical characteristics and looks they had on Earth.

Spirits can take the form of a lighter version of their earthly bodies, except that they always appear radiant, happy and healthy. There is no pain in Heaven, for pain is only an earthly concept, and they are free from the shackles we impose on ourselves in this life.

I can clearly remember a reading I once did, not too long ago, for a very kind and a gentle man, called Eddie - a great believer in the spiritual world.

It was a strange reading. Eddie had very few issues in his life, he was successful and happy with his world, but I felt he had come for a reading for a specific purpose. The reading was uneventful and I was disappointed that there wasn't something more that I could give him, beyond the confirmations I'd already passed along.

At the end of the reading he asked me about a friend named Mike that he hadn't seen in a long time; I immediately knew that his friend had died.

"Do you know that he is in spirit?" I asked.

Eddie nodded, he'd received word six months ago that his friend had died. He missed his friend very much and was sad that they hadn't spent much time together over the last few years, he was suffering from the same self-imposed guilt that many of us feel after a close friend or loved one dies.

He wanted to know if Mike was with him in spirit, and I told him that I could see a tall man but I wasn't getting his name.

I went on, to describe the spirit that I was seeing. Tall, brown hair, bright blue eyes and casually dressed. He had quite a sense of humor and loved practical jokes.

I spoke to Eddie, "He says he loves you and to let you know that he checks in on you from time to time." Eddie was still puzzled as to the identity of this unknown spirit.

Then I noticed that the spirit was showing me his deformed hand. I told Eddie, "He has a deformed hand."

Eddie drew in his breath, "That's Mike", he said as a tear rolled down his cheek. He later told me that his friend Mike had a deformed hand, and the confirmation that his good friend was now in spirit was comforting to him. Eddie went on in the world with his sense of calm restored.

I believe that spirits can suggest ideas or concepts to our sub-consciousness, ideas that just pop into our conscious minds as 'original' thoughts.

I'm sure that the real reason Eddie came to me for a reading was that his old friend Mike put the suggestion into his mind. Mike in spirit form just wanted to give his friend a sign of confirmation that he was still alive and well in the spirit world.

Spirits come in all shapes and forms. A friend of mine once told me about a young child spirit from the fairy realm that visited her from time to time.

One night, not too long after that discussion with my friend the spirit visited me while I was sleeping.

The image was so bright and intrusive that I awoke. As I opened my eyes the face of a little boy was hovering right in front of my face; I was frightened witless at the presence. I screamed and woke my husband and the spirit immediately vanished. Later, I realized that the spirit was simply like that of a small child who wakes a parent when they want something in the middle of the night.

We all wake up at some time with one of our children standing at our bedside and peering closely into our faces. Even though we know and love our children their sudden appearance is a disturbing shock.

Spirit Guides

Spirit Guides have previously incarnated a great number of times and have mastered all aspects of life on Earth. They have the experiences of life here and have been trained in the heavens for specific roles to assist humanity.

Spirits guides are not the same as angels. Angels were created by God for specific ethereal tasks whereas spirit guides are highly evolved souls that have taken on the job of helping people. Spirit guides have experience of life on Earth, they have lived as humans and so they can understand and relate to the earthly problems we have to contend with.

Evolved spirits, or spirit guides, return to Earth, not as ghosts - ghosts are wayward souls that haven't yet approached the pure white light of God's love - but as helpers and guides. They can manifest themselves to us.

Often spirit guides have a vocational aspect and are chosen to help us in specific ways. For example, a teacher or musician could have a guide that has previously incarnated and lived and worked as a teacher or musician. Therefore they understand the emotions and stress associated with those professions and felt by their human counterparts, their experience means they can better help us solve the problems we face here in this life.

Spirit guides are attracted to a soul and may follow that soul as it goes through a series of reincarnations. This process increases the bonding between our spirit guides and our earthly form.

I am blessed with many spirit guides that help me with my spiritual work: Claire, Korson, Samantha, and Abraham are just some of the guides that protect, help and encourage me as I strive to take God's message to a wider audience.

Even though actual manifestations themselves are initially intimidating, I feel special and so lucky that my guides physically appear before me.

Sometimes I wake up at night and find one of my helpers at my side. The room is lit brightly with a pulsating glow emanating from my visiting friend. After getting over the tremendous shock at having a visitor from the spiritual world in my bedroom I can relax and listen to the lessons and advice, gaining spiritual knowledge and comfort from the confirmations before me.

Our spirit guides are with us at all times. This is comforting, for we're never alone - we can always turn to our spirit guides for help and assistance. They love us unconditionally.

Spirit guides and our guardian angels are the small voice we hear within us. Softly counseling us, helping us to make decisions, giving us ideas and even warning us.

By listening to this guidance, we acknowledge them. By praying we invite God's helpers to continue to assist us. By giving thanks we honor them for their service to us.

She Talks with Angels

CHAPTER

12

PRAYER – COMMUNICATING WITH THE OTHER SIDE

*P*rayer is one of the main tools we can use to talk to God. By praying we can send messages into the spirit world, asking for help and guidance, seek comfort and send our thanks. We don't need rituals, a specific place or time to pray.

I can honestly say that throughout my life that each one of my prayers has been answered! Whatever I have given thanks for, I have received and my prayers for other people have been granted in wonderful ways.

Prayers should be profound messages from our soul to the higher realms. The wisest prayer of all is the one Jesus prayed, "Father all things are possible through you, let not my will be done, but what you will."

As humans we face many challenges. "Why is Life so hard?" we sometimes ask. I believe each one of us faces a crisis at some time in our lives, and the purpose of such major crises is to afford us an opportunity to turn to God.

We get so caught up in depending on others, for

emotional and physical support or even spiritually dependent on cult leaders - that we place too much importance in the messenger and not enough in the message. At a time of real crisis we can only find solace in God's love. We all experience periods of darkness during our life, they are important for only by that suffering can we learn the lessons and make the journey into the light.

In prayer we practice placing our problems with God. We must have faith and give up our attachments to human problems. In prayer we feel energized by God's white protective light, it helps remove us from our Earthly limitations.

Our prayers must be positive, simple, said with pure intent and sincerity, thank God and our angels for what we have, be thankful for our life and God's bounty.

When I pray I don't ask. When I want something for someone or myself I give thanks for that thing and see it as already done. My faith is strong and I know that God will answer my prayers because I have faith in God and myself. I believe I am worthy because my prayers are said with pure intent and I know God loves me. In prayer my intention is to help others find solutions to their problems through God. I send God's love to those I am praying for.

Prayers should not be repetitive; God hears us the

first time we pray, to keep reminding him of our needs infers we have little faith in his power.

Many people do not pray for themselves because they see themselves as unworthy or they carry tremendous guilt, maybe due to their own self-judgement. Some people are under the misconception that it is selfish to pray for themselves, because they believe that to be spiritual, they must put themselves last; all of those failings stem from a lack of self-love. God wants us to have it all. We are not meant to suffer or be martyrs while on our spiritual path.

God wants us to be whole, happy, healthy, loving, and fulfilled. We each have unlimited abilities. It is our belief system that gives us the freedom to create what ever we desire. Unfortunately, the societal and family values that we learn as we grow up, and religious beliefs affect us by setting self-imposed limitations on our thoughts and beliefs. Most of us buy into the idea that religions man-made rules are fact and we forget that man-made rules are just that, and no more.

It is important that we stay open to new possibilities and be grateful and positive to the opportunities that God sets in front of us. It is up to us individually to pray and then take action on the positive responses to our prayers.

Miracles through Prayer

People often ask me to pray for them or their loved ones. The only difference between my prayers and theirs, is my rock hard faith: I know the power of prayer can create miracles, for I see them frequently. So rather than pray for other people alone I also try to empower everyone by telling them to pray for themselves.

I consider myself as an instrument of God or as an extension of God and I utilize the gift of prayer to assist other people by bringing them solutions to their problems. Whether they are emotional or physical problems or helping them with financial, marital or family issues.

Some people believe I am a miracle worker because their problems seem to melt away when I pray for them. It is my belief in the power of God that comes through me to manifest miracles.

I have been blessed to see many miracles, both great and small. A lady called Sarah came to see me because she had a severe medical problem with one of her feet and the problems had progressed to the point that she could no longer walk on her bad foot. It had been weeks since her second laser surgery and her foot was not healing. She told me she had a large open wound on the ball of her foot.

In prayer I asked about Sarah's problems and relayed to her what I was told. The doctor had lasered too deeply and missed a section that should have been removed; now infection was setting in. She had tears in her eyes, for she was in pain with every step she took. She was turning to me for help. I asked her to remove the bandages so I could look at the wound, it was very deep and swollen. I told her to revisit her doctor and that I believed she actually needed more surgery. Well that was the last thing she wanted to hear and she started to cry.

During our time together, I silently asked the Archangel Rafael to assist me in healing Sarah's foot. She was in constant pain and it is hard to get through daily life without being able to walk. As she left that day I told her that I could see her walking normally again. This gave her hope.

A week later Sarah called to thank me, she said she didn't know what I did to her, but each day since she left my office she noticed her foot was healing. I told her I asked the Archangel Raphael to assist her in healing. Most of the time I pray for a healing without the person knowing about my request. I do this so they do not get in the way of the process.

Worthlessness, self-doubt, and negative thoughts all hinder the healing process. Several weeks later, I received a note of thanks from Sarah. She told me that her foot was completely healed and told me that I was now in her prayers!

*   *   *

I was walking in the mall one day with Patty, a friend of mine, and I noticed she was favoring one leg. She told me she was suffering from a severe reaction to a spider bite from two years earlier. She explained that after she had been bitten, blood poisoning had set in and red streaks appeared running up her leg.

Later, back at home she showed me her leg, it was very swollen and the area where she had been bitten had turned brown. The doctor told her there was nothing he could do and she was loosing the circulation in that leg.

I asked her permission to work on her. As I went into prayer the blessed mother came in to me and assisted me in healing Patty. I passed my hands up and down her leg and noticed that my hands were heating up, as always when I do healing work. Sometimes when I am doing a spiritual reading my hands start to radiate heat. This is the Great Spirit's way of telling me the person in front of me needs a physical healing.

As I worked on Patty she said she could feel tingling

in her leg. My whole body heated up and I was sweating. I worked hard to remove the poisons from her body. Patty had faith in me. She has seen me work before and knew that I have the gift of healing. During the healing she told me she could feel a difference. Not long after I saw her, the color was restored to the leg and it was no longer swollen! She was healed.

Mother's Prayers

Many women unknowingly bring sickness and tragedies to their children. Worrying is a concentrated negative thought. When dwelling on such negative thought consistently, we manifest those fears.

Wise is the mother that puts her child in God's hands. Thanking him for blessing and protecting the child. Never dwelling on negative possibilities, always visualizing her child happy, healthy and fulfilled.

A mother's prayers are very powerful and take precedence, being the first heard and answered because of their sincerity. A mother's prayer for a sick child should be positive. She should thank God for healing the child that was sick, not complain that her child is sick, for God already knows that, instead she should thank him for curing the child.

*   *   *

Guilt and fear can be a block to our prayers. Belief, faith and love are the tools we must use to overcome our human limitations. If we pray just from fear or insincerity we waste our time, our prayers must be said with faith. Worrying is like praying for something negative to happen.

The human mind is a very powerful tool in prayer and meditation. Use the mind to visualize what you are asking for. See yourself gaining the attributes you are looking for. Visualization and faith in action can manifest your prayers into reality.

Our prayers can be a powerful healing agent when used to help another person, a group of people, or even a troubled location (such as the rainforest) here on earth.

The power of prayer is magnified greatly when groups of people pray at the same time and positively give thanks for the solution to a prayer that will be answered. Group Prayers are immeasurably powerful and have the ability to manifest a miracle.

Group prayers saved my cousin from a certain death from two vicious strains of leukemia. Consigned to a terminal illness by his medical experts my cousin was resigned to his imminent death. Determined to save his young life, Church and family prayer groups linked with others around the world and gave thanks for his full recovery. Miraculously, my cousin soon went into full remission. Doctors were astounded by his recovery and were unable to offer any medical explanations for his continued good health.

The spirit world not only hears our prayers but they are seen also. Imagine being out in space looking down on the planet Earth. Our prayers look like bright beams of light projected from Earth out into the Universe. We project our thoughts of pure intent out into the heavens. We are truly more powerful than we know.

The pure intent of prayer can make a difference; I have seen it many times.

I went with a group of ten people to a family style restaurant. The food was served in large bowls and passed around the table and shared by all. Silently I blessed my food. The next day I started to receive phone calls, eight people out of the ten were sick with a slight case of food poisoning. I didn't feel any ill effects from the bad food.

Similarly, when there is contamination of a water source, why do some town residents get sick and some not?

Prayer, Faith and your personal belief system play an important part of our well being.

The power of prayer cannot be overstated, it is the single most powerful method we have in this world to regain contact with the spirit world. Use prayer and benefit with answers to the questions you seek.

We must remember that prayers are not just getting on our knees, but positive thoughts also act as prayers. When we wish some one well, we are sending them love and with love it is followed by God's white protective light. Our thoughts are prayers too.

Gratitude is an essential ingredient of prayer, because without gratitude our prayers are meaningless. Being thankful and concentrating on your blessings will create abundance, prosperity, and more blessings. It is important that we acknowledge and appreciate God and his legion of helpers. In thankfulness, God's love is continually bestowed upon us and we are demonstrating our faith.

Never Limit A Prayer

It is important to communicate with God and our spirit helpers each day. Speak to them, as they are your best friends. Tell them about the issues you are faced with. Be specific about problems, but do not attempt to tell them how to fix your problems. When we make this mistake we limit our prayers.

As in life, we set our own limitations in prayer. Sometimes, we can be presumptuous in our prayers and tell God how to fix our problems. This limits the solutions, for God knows the divine answers to all our earthly problems.

Like the old proverb; "Be careful what you wish for, you just may get it." God knows what is in our best interest. God knows what we need, whereas we know only what we want. Most of the time we are only asking for a slice of cake when God would be glad to give us the whole cake!

I always allow God the freedom to find the solution that is for the highest good of all involved. I believe that God will give me the best solution to a problem if I allow him that freedom. They can always do more for us than we can imagine. I hand my problems over to God and ask him to take care of it. He will always give me the perfect solution. He has never failed me.

Blessing Food

Blessing food we are about to eat is a ritual that has slipped away from our tables in today's speed filled society, yet the blessing of food is now more important than ever.

The over-processed foods in our fast paced lifestyles are full of chemicals. These chemicals are added to food in the manufacturing process supposedly to make it taste more palatable, lengthen the shelf life and make the food look more appetizing on the store shelves.

Scientists have altered the genetics of the plants we eat for their nutrients to feed our physical bodies. They have altered them to make them bigger, withstand strains of plant diseases and to make them more eye appealing. These mutant plants no longer produce seed that will germinate, they cannot recreate their own species.

Prayer has the power to transform anything we place in our mouths for the purpose of sustenance. The food is purified by our intent.

We should pray before we begin to consume any meal and bless the food in any manner in which we are comfortable. Address the Great Spirit, thank her for the abundance of Mother Earth. Thank the animal that gave its life to provide nutrition for you. Thank God for blessing and purifying the food that is generously provided.

***Every visible thing in
this world is put in
the charge of an Angel.***

– Saint Augustine

MEDITATION – CONNECTING TO THE SOURCE

*M*editation is a tool we can employ to connect with our angels and spirit guides, it is a listening tool, allowing a one sided conversation with the spirit world. It is a time for us to receive spiritual messages.

As we learn to walk and talk, so must we learn the proper way to meet with God. Our bodies are composed of three parts: mental, physical and spiritual. We must attune all parts of ourselves to be balanced spiritual beings.

Our mind is the builder of our self-created future. We cannot obtain what we cannot see ourselves worthy of receiving. We should think positively about all things, this is a virtue. We should edit our thoughts, consciously erasing the negative from our mind.

Our physical body is our temple, it is the vessel that holds our soul. Keeping it clean, working properly and free of impurities is important.

Our soul or our God-part-self is the essence of our

being that we project into the higher realms when we meditate or while in prayer. Through consistent communing with God we can expand our consciousness, that way our spiritual knowledge and our connection to God increases.

Through centering our attention on God we gain a sense of peace and love, - flowing from higher dimensions. This union gives us a source of inner strength.

When meditation is practiced daily we change. Negative habits will drop away, to be replaced with confidence and harmony. In many cases meditation gives way to a sense of self-awareness and in turn can then help us overcome disease. This is energy that vitalizes us and opens us to a new sense of oneness with the universe. Instead of identifying ourselves with our illness we become aware that our state of mind controls our ability to change the physical condition.

We are multidimensional beings; everything we create is created first in the spirit realm, and then followed in the physical plane. Meditating regularly heightens our sense of perception.

Meditation is the conscious effort of withdrawing our attention from physical activities and mental distractions to center our attention seeking God. Our minds are constantly active, life, jobs, children, ambitions and desires all crowd each other, in an endless circle. We have to push away those earthly emotions and concentrate on emptying our minds, clearing the mind and detaching from the body.

Meditation isn't easy to accomplish at first. To successfully meditate we must let our mind recede to the edge of our consciousness and connect with our higher self. When we can achieve this state by relaxation we have 'quieted the mind.'

I believe it is now easier to get in touch with the spirit world than at any other time in mankind's history. There is a joining together of mankind and the spirit world as God makes it easier for each of us to open our hearts and minds to him.

This is a very special time in the history of the Earth, there is now a vibrational shift which allows us to make direct contact with the spirit world. God is ready to help, but we have to approach him first and ask for that help.

Meditation is a tool we can use. We no longer have to undergo special rituals or employ special methods, we simply have to clear all the day to day trivia from our minds and open the door to our Angels and Spirit Guides.

To be a good listener we must tune out our own ego and conscious mind, allowing access to our higher mind. Meditation is a way we can listen to the messages from within ourselves that come from our soul's connection to God.

Spirits don't shout at us, they just create a feeling, a thought, or a mental picture for us. Their input is subtle and quiet, but if we listen carefully enough we can all experience the feelings of total awareness and love that they impart to us as they relay messages.

*   *   *

I meditate by laying in a quiet room and concentrate on relaxing my body. When my mind is clear I can then start the relaxation process.

I start by relaxing my toes, then move up to my feet, ankles, legs and so on until I feel completely at peace and empty, letting my mind rest on the easy rhythm of my breathing.

The way we breathe is critical. To achieve complete relaxation and help ease our bodies and minds into a state of deep meditation we must breathe correctly.

My personal breathing technique that invariably works for me is to breathe in deeply through my nose and take the air into my diaphragm and hold that breath for a few seconds before exhaling through my mouth. I continue this breathing exercise until I reach a state of detachment, a state of deep meditation.

It is important that we concentrate on our regulated

breathing because this concentration helps distract the conscious mind from the day to day trivia.

Sometimes the relaxation process, the pre-cursor to meditation doesn't work at the first try. For example I may be feeling particularly stressed or may be distracted by a phone call, car horn, kids, or other outside influences. When this happens I simply start the relaxation process over again and continue until I'm fully relaxed.

Mind chatter is a common distraction. Thoughts tend to stream through our mind. When mind chatter continues don't fight it or deny it. The more you fight it, the more it persists. You have all the time in the world. Let the thoughts flow. They will stop.

When my mind is clear, I then have opened the door to my higher self and can let the information and messages flow into me from the spirit world.

Some people find it more assuring when they meditate to ask for a sign from their Guides and Angels. The spirits will often respond and provide a sign of confirmation.

Angels and Spirit Guides are subtle. Spirit guides remember their time on Earth and remember the fear of the unknown that weighed on their minds. If a spirit appeared before us when we pray or meditate, then most people would be shocked and scared.

The Spirit Guide understands this and so chooses, certainly when we first connect with them, to give us subtle signs. These signs vary, perhaps a feeling of warmth and love washes over us, some people say they feel a presence in the room when they meditate, others report a fresh fragrance or an unseen hand lightly brushing and stroking their hair.

Confirmation can be answered with noise, a voice calling your name or the sound of heavenly instrumental music that seems to come out of thin air.

All the signs are confirmations, a break through to this world, to let us know that our prayers and meditations are working and being received 'loud and clear' by our Guardian Angels and Spirit Guides.

When you are looking for a specific answer to a current problem focus your thoughts on that issue and listen for the response from your Angels and Spirit Guides.

Meditation is a powerful communication tool, practice and improve your skills, you will be rewarded with the ability to speak with your personal attendants and helpers from the spirit world. You will feel peace and love wash over you and be ready to face the world with renewed vigor, energy and hope. For you will be confident that your path through life is a happy one.

The importance of meditation cannot be over stressed. It allows us to develop spiritually by raising our consciousness and vibration and to receive direct guidance from God.

DREAMS – A WINDOW TO THE SPIRIT WORLD

*O*ur dreams play an important role in our life. If we live to be 70 years old we will have spent more than 200,000 nights asleep in our beds, in all we sleep through about one third of our life.

During our sleeping time we rest, heal and recharge our spirit, but often it's the time when our spirit is the most active. Our sleep time provides an opportunity for our spirit to leave our body and refresh itself in the spirit world. For many people their dreams are the nearest they get to the spirit world while still living in this world.

All people dream when they are asleep, those dreams are very important because they represent another opportunity for us to contact the spirit world.

Often our spirits live out actions and events that we are going to encounter in this life - we have a 'dry run' of things to come in our conscious life. So dreams are our window to the spirit world and our own future.

More importantly it is "Spirit's" way of initiating

contact with us, for while we sleep we are relaxed and our minds are open and receptive. No prejudices or constraints limit our ability to absorb information when we sleep. This is the time that spirits choose to approach, when we are at our most receptive.

Only last month during a private reading for a lady, her mother's spirit came in to tell me that she loved her daughter very much and that her youngest daughter, my client's sister, needed her help. The other sister was going through some difficult times and needed love and assurance that everything would be fine and the problems would be resolved. The mother had been visiting the younger sister in her dreams, giving her comfort and love to ease her distress.

After the reading was finished I counseled my client to ask her sister if she had been dreaming recently about her mother.

Sure enough, the other sister confirmed that since her own troubles had begun she had frequently dreamt of her mother who appeared in her dreams with comforting messages.

The experiences of my client and her sister demonstrate that spirits are constantly coming to our aid in times of danger or stress. Frequently, a spirit approaches when we are asleep and in our dream time to help another.

Dreams are not imaginary, nor are they illusions;

they are actual events, situations, and meetings that our souls go through while our bodies lie asleep in bed. The world of dreams is the real world, and our waking lives are merely an illusion.

When we sleep only our conscious mind rests. Our spirit can sometimes leave us temporarily and move into the spirit world; this is called an 'out of body experience', these experiences can result in dramatic changes to our perceptions and ourselves.

I am blessed with an evolved soul that has advanced to a higher spiritual ranking, and I can recall most events that happen during my dream time.

I know that when I am asleep my soul leaves my body to do spiritual work with other souls. This work includes healing, teaching and lecturing.

'Astral travel' is a name we give to a journey the soul takes while the physical body is resting. The traveling of the soul into different dimensions, whether on Earth, other planets or in the astral realms.

Everyone has these out of body experiences, conscious or unconscious, frequently throughout their life. As the body rests, the mind wanders and the person place or thing that you are thinking about as you drift off to sleep, then the soul goes to that place or person.

We remember those trips as dreams but be assured we were really there.

The subconscious mind acts as a filter based on our belief system or our fears. The conscious mind will not allow us to remember subconscious memories that do not coincide with our beliefs.

During their dream, time many people experience feelings of bird-like flight and when they wake they remember all the wonderful sensations of flying. Those sensations were not just dreams, the soul was on a journey and this memory of flying was a portion of what was actually experienced in the spirit realm. You were really flying!

Some people have mastered the art of astral travel. They have taught themselves to will their soul to leave the body and travel to a destination, while they are consciously controlling and experiencing the trip.

There are many reasons the soul travels while the body sleeps. For example some go to check on a loved one they are worried about. Many times while I am out of town doing TV interviews or a workshop in another city I will astral travel home at night to check on my children. Then consciously or unconsciously the soul astral traveling knows that person they are worried about is fine.

Another reason the soul leaves is to return to the spirit world and interact with other souls we care about. In this realm we can do anything. We can visit with a loved one who has died. We are also able to hang out and do things with our friends and family still living. We can also work out problems and issues with others in the spirit realm and we connect with our Spirit Guides and Angels for direction and help. Most people remember bits and pieces of these visits as dreams.

As the body sleeps we return to the heavens to rest and heal our soul. This soul rejuvenation can only take place where God's love and light exist in its purest form...in the spirit world. Sleeping has always been thought to be needed for the physical body but actually sleep is primarily needed for the soul.

Astral traveling is the way our spirit has freedom. The soul is not confined to our man-made physical limitations. We are able to see other parts of the Earth, visit with family and friends, see other worlds, astral planes, or even do God's work.

Some souls actually have jobs they perform while the physical body sleeps. Soul retrieval is a job done in spirit, one soul helping another to move into the heavens. There are many spiritual jobs such as healing or teaching that are performed while we sleep. We are not only able to learn here on the Earth in our physical bodies, but our souls also continue to be active as we sleep.

When the soul returns from astral travel we

sometimes feel the sensation of falling or a big jolt as we wake up. We get this sensation when our soul rejoins our body in a hurry. This happens if someone is trying to wake us, our sleep is interrupted, or if we have encountered something unpleasant or fearful, we automatically return to the body.

Many people wake up with vivid memories after an out of body experience, because the spirit has actually undergone an experience so profound that the memory not only carries into the conscious mind but can cause measurable changes to heartbeat, respiration, adrenaline flow and brain wave patterns.

While dreaming we can also experience past life memories. People, events and places from different historical periods that we recall in our dream state reflect our earlier lives in those situations.

We can dream of events, situations and people, these dreams are real. When we are awake and our mind is full of the here and now we close out the other world. When we sleep we dream and we unconsciously open the doorway to the spirit world.

While dreaming we live out events and incidents that we are going to experience in our conscious state. The dream is a premonition of things to come in this world. In the Dream State we can work out real world solutions to problems as we act out events and situations in our dreams.

I always counsel people to keep a record of their dreams, keep a dream journal and write down everything you remember - as soon as you awake. Make notes before climbing from bed, otherwise critical elements of the dream will be lost as the conscious mind blocks out the dreamscape.

Over time, the journal notes will become more detailed and accurate as you train your conscious mind to record your dreams.

Some people prefer to keep a tape recorder at the side of their bed ready for instant recording while the dreams are still fresh in their minds. Listening to old dream tapes can help us can work out solutions that were presented to us in the dream time.

Dreams offer us a great potential tool for communicating with the other world. We should each make use of our dreams and pay attention to the lessons we can learn from them.

Dream premonitions are a way for Angels and Spirit Guides to communicate with us, for in the dream state we are receptive to spiritual thoughts. Our soul receives advance warning of impending danger or dangerous situations and those messages are passed to us as premonitions.

Many people dream of dead family members,

relatives, and friends, loved ones, and even pets. Those dreams are visits from the spirits of those people or animals that have visited us while we are asleep. They come and calm our fears, help us work through unhappy times, resolve problems and let us know they are at peace and waiting patiently to greet us when we cross the threshold.

I believe some of those dream state visitors come along to us from love or friendship and just 'drop in' for a chat and a friendly conversation.

Astral travel is a truly wondrous journey that we can all undertake. To help you take your own astral journey I've laid out some guidelines:

Many people fall asleep when they first start experimenting with astral travel as the meditation and relaxation lull the body into sleep.

The trick is to catch yourself, and remain aware as you go into the next dimension or the Dream State. I always recommend initially trying it in the afternoon, for then the body is not exhausted and ready for a good night's sleep.

First pick your target location, lay flat on your back and start to meditate by relaxing your body and concentrating on your breathing. Relax the entire body while willing yourself to your destination.

It is best not to have eaten before attempting the

astral travel; the digestion of food uses much of the energy that we need to use in traveling.

Think of planning a trip and try to concentrate without interruptions; feel yourself floating. You will hear a slight buzzing in your ear or even the sensation of vibration. You may see yourself floating above your bed. Now is the time to focus on your destination, we travel at the speed of our thoughts.

There is no need to worry, your lighter body is still connected to the physical body by a silver cord. God has given us built in protection. This silver cord is like an umbilical cord. Your lighter body looks just like you but is more transparent, as is the silver cord. The only time the cord is severed is at the point of death, this severance releases the soul from the physical plane.

Example of Astral Travel

Once I had mastered consciously willing myself to astral travel I decided I wanted some proof and confirmation that I wasn't merely dreaming.

I wanted someone I knew to see me, and so confirm to me that my soul was actually traveling to a destination of my choosing.

This was a challenge for me not only to go to a specific location but also to manifest myself so someone could see me. I chose a close friend's house as a target destination because I wanted to be sure I was traveling to a safe environment.

I lay in bed in the early hours of the morning and began to meditate, relaxing and concentrating on my breathing envisioning my friend's house. Becoming completely relaxed I felt the start of the familiar hum and slight vibrations that I experience when my soul leaves my body. Within seconds I looked down and saw my physical body resting in my bed, and I was free!

I soared up into the starry sky like a bird, flying fast and gazing down at rooftops. That feeling of complete freedom gave me a sense of overwhelming joy.

Quickly, I moved to my friend's familiar neighborhood, onto her front door and I dove right through it. I found her sleeping soundly in her bed.

Now I concentrated my thoughts on making myself visible. Using the power of my mind and focusing intently on creating a denser body I tried to wake her up. Finally, her eyes fluttered, then opened slightly and she gave me a small grin then went back to a sound sleep. I knew she had seen me, her smile told me that.

The next day, she stopped by my home and we sat down in the kitchen, just having a regular conversation. She said to me there's something I wanted to tell you, but now I can't remember what it was.

'Great' I thought to myself 'I want some confirmation'.

"I saw you last night! I woke up and saw you at the foot of my bed. I thought I was dreaming, but then I realized you really were there." She looked stunned to have remembered the experience with such vivid recall.

Yes, finally I had confirmation! I could astral travel to a place of my choosing and make my presence known to a witness at the other end.

Now I knew I had to practice and perfect this new tool and pass along the unique benefits and experiences to others.

Comas

When a body is in a coma the soul has left the physical body and traveled to another place. When there is physical trauma to a body this departure will induce a coma because the soul has been thrown from the body. The silver cord connection to the soul keeps the physical body alive. The coma patient does not feel pain.

When we are under the effects of anesthesia our soul automatically disconnects from the body. There are many documented cases of patients relaying details of their entire surgery and even conversations that took place while their body was under anesthesia and the soul was hovering overhead watching from above.

Our eternal soul is an amazing thing. Whether we are meditating, dreaming, astral traveling, or in a coma, when the mind detaches from the physical body, the soul automatically knows its way home to the heavens.

**And he dreamed and
behold a ladder set up on Earth,
and the top of it reached Heaven,
and behold the Angels of God
ascending and descending on it.**

– Genesis 28

AURAS – THE COLOR OF OUR ENERGY

*O*ur physical body ticks along for years and years. We each have a heartbeat and a pulse. Our diaphragm moves and our lungs pump air in and out. We see, hear and communicate interactively with the rest of the world. But what is the 'spark' that brings us to life, what makes each of us tick?

The soul is the essence that makes the body live and thrive. Take away the soul and our body stops living. The soul or essence is joined to the body by a link called the 'Silver Cord'.

As every living being has a soul, so every living being has an aura, the aura is the energy field radiating from the soul. Auras can be seen around a person's body, a light field shimmering with color and energy.

We can see the soul by viewing a person's aura. Their very essence can be seen as color, vibration or a pulsing light.

The aura, sometimes called the "Over Soul" contains different colors, white represents our soul, but other colors can often be seen.

Gifted psychics can read the energy from an aura and determine a soul's ranking and past lives. A soul's history is contained within the aura.

The colors represent the condition of our soul and our general health. Psychics can differentiate from the different colors in an aura a specific illness that afflicts a person.

The strength or weakness of the aura's pulsation is another indicator of health and a soul's condition. Strong vibrant pulsations that reach out from the body indicate a strong and powerful energy and a content soul whereas a weakly pulsating aura will usually be dark colored and indicative of illness or extreme tiredness.

Black or dark gray auras represent ill health, someone who may be seriously ill, or very run down and tired. Then the aura may not reach out, it seems to pulse close to the person's body. This indicates that they need to recharge their physical and ethereal batteries. Those people will benefit from prayer and meditation, they need to open up their minds and hearts to God and their Guardian Angels, then they will become recharged and refreshed.

At times an aura can be felt before it is seen. Like an energy source, auras can be felt as heat, a warmth, or by vibrations. It radiates from our body. For example:

without reason you feel uncomfortable with someone you just met and you have a subconscious feeling of dislike. It can be that your energy is not compatible with this new person's energy.

Another time we feel a strong aura is when someone invades our personal space. Often we experience this when a person comes very close to us and we have the need to take a step backward. We are subconsciously removing them from our aura or energy field.

*   *   *

Almost everybody can learn to see and read auras. It is not a closed secret only available to mediums and psychics.

Every living thing has an essence or soul and we can learn to read them all. Plants, trees, animals - even rocks have auras that can be read with practice.

To learn how to read an aura takes effort, patience and practice. I always recommend that you start by reading auras in this way:

Ask a friend or partner to stand perfectly still against a blank wall in a semi-darkened room.

Concentrate on the area outlining the person - don't look at them directly - look around them or above the head.

Sometimes you will see a faint pulsating light or a

brighter light in the air around the person. With enough practice and meditation you will see a glimpse of light or color, as you study the energy just above the persons head. With practice, aura watching becomes easier until over time you can see an aura almost at will.

Prayer and meditation are important tools. Relax and tune out your own ego and conscious thought, then when you are receptive to the spirit world it will be easier for you to see somebody else's aura.

Some people practice by reading the aura surrounding a tree. They go out at nighttime or dusk and concentrate on the tree, whilst freeing their minds from conscious thought. A tree usually has a faint white aura, very faint, but it's there to be seen.

Personally, I have a very strong aura. Many people find it easy to read my aura as it bursts out of my physical body. Others feel the heat and energy emanating from my essence.

Auras have been photographed. Many years ago a Russian scientist invented a unique form of photography, now called Kierlian photography. This technique allows the camera to capture the energy waves emanating from a human body.

Eastern cultures use the life essence or energy in different ways. Proponents of the martial arts and tai chi use the chi or 'energy of life' and can actually project their energy towards other people to protect themselves from danger.

The Light - Our Spark of God

The aura is 'The light'. It is an essence that is contained within our soul, it is the spark of God that resides within us all. It is the light that radiates from inside us...reflecting outward as the over-soul. Look inside any of us and you will see the light within, the pure white light of God.

In times of fear and danger we can call upon God's white protective light and wrap it around us like an invincible armor of love, to protect us from negativity and emotional harm.

Mediums and psychics can look at people's life force and physically see their essence represented as a white light. When looking at babies and toddlers their aura is spectacular. You can see a bright beam of white light that shoots up from the heart, through their crown and into the air. This connection represents the child's purity and receptiveness to God. Young children are clearly connected to the spirit world.

THE CHILDREN – OUR FUTURE

*C*reation of life is one of the wonders of our known universe, but when is life actually created?

Humans reproduce and create children; a complex mix of DNA and genes determine gender, racial characteristics, personality traits and some argue, our lifespan.

During the period of gestation, when a baby is growing in the mothers womb, it is merely a biological appendage, a fetus that can be measured and quantified by biologists, something that can be reproduced in a test tube and inserted into a host's womb.

That growing specimen only becomes a human being, an addition to mankind, when a Soul enters the baby's body. At, or before, the moment of birth, the baby takes a life of its own as the Soul enters and completes the last dynamic cycle needed to sustain life and produce a sentient being. A new life with its own free will is created and born.

The innocence of a newborn baby are evident by its

sweet smell of purity. All mothers are familiar with this scent. This smell is a direct link to the heavens. As we grow the scent of purity disappears.

Many argue that abortion is not the taking of a life, because the fetus does not have a life or will of its own, until the Soul conjoins with the body at the time of birth. Thus abortion is the removal of a fetus, that may be able to physically sustain life, but has not yet been blessed with a Soul. As a psychic I can clearly see the soul of a child hovering around its intended mother. The removal of a fetus is biological. All souls are eternal.

*   *   *

Children represent the future of both mankind and the Earth, they are our physical link into the future, and represent a link to our immediate past.

All too often, our young children give us signs and messages that we ignore, simply because we are adults and believe ourselves wiser. Parents should spend time listening to their children, for they often demonstrate undeniable links to the spirit world.

Many children develop 'make-believe friends' that adults just ignore as a part of a child's fantasy. We are wrong to do that, our children's imaginary friends are not imaginary at all... they are visitors from the spirit world, angels, spirit guides, loved ones and fairies, spirits that exist on another plane and are invisible to our eyes.

Take a closer look at these imaginary friends that children see, talk and play with. These friends never lead our children into harm's way, rather they nurture them, keep them company and protect them from harm.

I believe that the so called fantasy friends are the manifestations of a child's Guardian Angels and spirit guides, who appear to the child and act as companions on adventures unknown and forgotten by adults. The child can readily see and interact with the Angels and spirits. Yet we only see the child talking with him or herself, and think nothing more of it, yet if an adult were to do the same thing, they would be committed to a mental institute in a flash.

The truth is that our lives are crowded with grown up problems, paying the mortgage and car payments, pressures of work, keeping up with the Jones' and the biggest fear of all, the consuming fear of death. Young children don't have those pressures; their minds are open and receptive, not yet clouded with prejudices or pre-conceived ideas and opinions.

They don't filter out, analyze or rationalize any suggestions or messages that pop up in their minds, rather they accept what they see and hear at face value. Isn't it then natural that our children can see and talk with Spirits while most adults cannot?

We traded our ability to talk with our Spirit Guides and Angels for maturity and pleasures of the flesh, the here and now. In doing so, we closed our minds to the perceived 'unnatural' approaches from our own Angels.

All too often we dismiss subjects that we don't understand, topics that are unknown and threaten our perception of the world. Children haven't yet adopted our values or the mental growth that we force on them and they benefit from that. They can do things many adults have lost the ability to do, they can talk with Angels.

When a child tells a parent about an imaginary adult who talks with them and strokes their hair, do they really refer to a visit from the Spirit of a departed grandparent or other near relative?

Sometimes a child can make what adults think of as a shocking revelation. They may describe a person or place or event that we, as adults, know happened before they were born or in a place they've never visited. Scared of the underlying truth in these messages, parents too quickly try and rationalize the stories or discredit them, never to be spoke of again.

The truth is that our children are receiving visits from Spirits, Spirits they can see as clearly as we see each other, on the physical plane. These loving spirits talk with our children and impart them with knowledge way beyond their years.

Other times children may see glimpses into their own past lives and recall events that happened before they entered this world of here and now.

Many mediums believe that we incarnate at least 60 times. Our soul has lived and breathed on this little planet many times. Is it so unusual that a child can see glimpses of one of those earlier incarnations?

There are many documented accounts of 'miracle' children who act in apparently bizarre ways. The young children with no knowledge of music who faithfully reproduce the music of long dead composers such as Chopin and Beethoven. Yet another wrote long treatises about political life in the 18th century and another accurately described medical procedures that left professional surgeons dumbfounded.

There are no logical or rational explanations for these strange events. Parents often do not wish to show off their offspring as a freakshow and so closet them away in private schools, away from the prying eyes of the media.

It's the parents who are really scared of the unknown, afraid to acknowledge that their children are different from the majority - for today's society is gray and to stand out can be dangerous.

Those children whose bodies host an older soul are

different - for those children are happy with their abilities. The children aren't fazed, because they know the truth and are willing to embrace it.

Only when we, the adults, face the issues children present can we accept that Spirits connect and communicate with children in ways that seem lost to us. We need to get back to basic values and open our minds, and perhaps then we too will all be able once again to talk with Angels.

*   *   *

Many writers recognize children's ability to see things beyond the understanding of adults. So a form of specialized fiction, storybooks have been developed. They emulate the process of a child's mind and finds there an understanding audience; trees and animals, trains and boats that live and talk with children, fantasy worlds that mirror our existence and places populated by the forces of good - that always overcome the forces of bad.

We even name the characters that our children have to deal with elves, fairies, gnomes, the little people, goblins, bogeymen and so on. These aren't fantasy creations. They are spirits from the Fairy Realm. They exist just as surely as we do. We all remember that fairies live at the bottom of the garden in a shady glen and that elves live under toadstools. When did we learn for sure that they don't?

These names and ideas have been handed down as folklore from generation to generation for thousands of years. But social historians know that a lot folklore was based on fact, from times when adults too were more open and receptive with unclouded minds. Perhaps if we lived in those long lost days, we too would have thought it normal to openly converse with Angels, Fairies and with our own Spirit Guides.

*   *   *

Studies have shown that many young children, as well as musicians, have a marked Extra Sensory Perception (ESP) and telepathic abilities, knowledge that hasn't been taught to them by any adult; the children were born with those natural skills.

By the age of eight those skills fade away until they are lost in the subconscious, as the child becomes more aware of worldly attractions; TV, peer pressures and targeted marketing campaigns. Everything that's calculated to grab children's attention and rush them into a too early materialistic view of life.

Parents are often guilty of pushing their children

into growing up and urge them to quickly leave behind the childish ideas of life. In doing so, parents encourage their children to abandon childhood values and openness. The children close their minds and become fixated on competing and winning to the extent that they lose the ability to see and interact with their own imaginary friends.

Those mind agility and strength skills then lie unused for so long that they wither and nearly die, sometimes not completely forgotten, but pushed into the far reaches of the mind where they lie dormant for years. As adults those memories sometimes awaken at times of great stress or shock.

We can also get back in touch with our angels and spirits through the power of prayer, meditation and our nightly dreams. Although we have to first accept their existence and have faith in God and his love for each of us.

*   *   *

A few spiritually enlightened children, called 'Blue Ray' or 'Indigo Children', started appearing on earth about ten years ago, a development that continues today, with ever increasing numbers of these children being born around the world. These children show signs of a higher spiritual evolution, they are the beginning of the next link in the evolution of the human species. These children are born with particularly strong remembrances of their spiritual self and past lives. They are aware of heaven and God's infinite wisdom and goodness well before they reach an age of awareness in this life.

Some people theorize that these special children hold the key to secrets about the interaction of mankind with the spirit world, so far known only to a few gifted psychics and prophets.

Our children should be looked at and listened to with a special care. Angels and Spirit Guides talk to our children, and they'll talk with each of us - all we have to do is open the door to our consciousness and let them into our lives.

When I lecture in bookstores, I find it especially rewarding to see young faces in the audience. I believe that children who gravitate towards the lecture area to hear me speak are more spiritually aware than many adults and their peers.

Once I noticed a very special girl, of about twelve years old, watching and listening intently in the audience as I talked about Guardian Angels.

At the end of a lecture, sometimes my helpers in spirit direct me to give messages to members of the audience and that day was no exception. As I passed through the front rows of seats, I was given information for this little girl.

I turned and told her that her Angel was telling me she was to become a doctor. Not just an ordinary doctor, but one destined to help millions of people through a cure she would discover.

She listened to me with a slight smile on her face and when I finished recounting the message from her Angel, she thanked me with a knowing look then confirmed that she has always wanted to be a doctor. I knew that this was a young girl who is destined to go far in this life by fulfilling her spiritual mission.

*   *   *

Many times mothers come to me for readings specifically for information to help their children. Sometimes these women don't know why they are moved to request a reading. The motivation has come from outside them, a spirit has placed the thought in their subconscious, because the spirit world has a message for them.

During one such reading for a mother, I was shocked to clearly see a toddler drowning in a lake. Quickly I cautioned the mother that the vision was a warning from the child's Guardian Angel.

I was emphatic and believe I scared the mother, but sometimes it takes a good fright to motivate someone to move in the right direction.

I knew that the premonition of the drowning toddler was preventable, if it were the child's destiny to drown, then there would be no warning.

Therefore, I instinctively knew that with a little caution and some preventative measures this child's life could be saved. I counseled the mother to put the child through swim classes and to be very observant whenever the child was around water.

Months later, the mother called to thank me, she had a story to relate that ended well, but without my premonition and warning could have had terrible consequences.

She told me her two sons and her husband had spent the day at a park. The boys were playing by the water and the father was lying on a beach towel watching them. The father was distracted by a volleyball game and turned his head away for a few moments. Just at that second, the smaller son stumbled in the water, fell and disappeared under the surface. The older boy turned around and noticed his little brother missing. He screamed for help.

The father ran to the water and searched the spot where his son was last seen. Thrashing about in the murky water, he bumped into the boy, who was on the bottom. Quickly, he pulled his son from the water and carried him onto the beach. The boy's life was saved and he continues to live a normal and healthy life.

The mother thanked me for my earlier help and insistence that the family watch the boy carefully when he was near water. The father was aware of my warning, and even though he had been momentarily distracted, he was subconsciously ready to spring into immediate action as soon as he heard the scream of distress from his son.

*We are like children,
who stand in the need of masters to
enlighten and direct us,
and God has provided this,
by appointing His Angels
to be our teachers and guides.*

– Saint Thomas Aquinas

ANIMAL TOTEMS

In spirit we each have Animal Totems that represent a teaching or power, they are spiritual characteristics that influence us in our daily lives.

As we have two Guardian Angels, we also have two Animal Totems that are with us at all times. In times of need, crisis or emotional stress other Animal Totems can offer us guidance.

They are connected to Mother Earth, the fairy realm and the earth angels. In our everyday life animals unfamiliar to us can cross our paths, when these unusual events occur we know that Mother Earth is talking to us and sending us a message.

For example, a young woman was talking to some friends when five owls landed nearest to her. Owls are nocturnal creatures so this was surely a sign. Her Native American friends were astounded at the powerful sign. The owl is sometimes an omen of death or danger. Within six months the sign had clearly proved to have been a warning, four of her family members had died since the time of the warning. Mother Nature was speaking to her, giving her advanced warning to prepare herself for death.

Another time, a woman I know in South Florida was driving to work in the city in the early dawn hours when she suddenly noticed three monkeys crossing the road in front of her car.

This sighting was unusual in itself, but what made it seem bizarre was that the woman spotted them again the next morning.

She called me and explained what had happened. I told her the two events were almost certainly a message from Mother Earth and that she should pay more attention to her family.

*   *   *

Native Americans believe each animal has a unique medicine or power to offer. You will find that your personal Animal Totems gravitate to you in the physical as well as in the Spirit World. By meditating on a particular animal you can find solutions to your problems.

I have included the basic definitions of the various animal totems below:

Eagle - Great Spirit: This majestic bird represents

God and unlimited possibilities. The ability to see the bigger picture.

Hawk - The Messenger: The bringer of news and warnings, telling of things to come. Hawk is a protector of the physical body and the spirit, and will follow you on your journey.

Elk - Stamina: The teacher of endurance, learning to pace yourself and maintain wellness of the body. It represent the cycles and seasons of life.

Deer - Gentleness: Represents unconditional love. It teaches us to be kind to our brothers and sisters by setting the example.

Bear - Introspection: To retreat within and reflect. The protector of women and children. The ability to work out problems in the dream-time and astral realms. Intuition.

Snake - Transmutation: The sexual and spiritual energy that comes from the same source. Kundalini Energy. Healing abilities and magical gifts.

Otter - Healer: Female energies of creativeness, intuition, and sharing. Knowledge of holistic medicine and remedies; The Medicine Woman.

Butterfly - Change of State: Transformation, the journey of the soul. Represents the process of creation and manifestation.

Turtle - Mother Earth: The female energy of Birth, balance, grounding, and patience.

Coyote - Trickster: The art of self-sabotage. The learning of life's lessons the hard way. The humorous deceiver. A survivor.

Dog - Loyalty and Faithfulness: Represents being in the service of others. Working for humanity. Unconditional love.

Wolf - Teacher: The communicator, lecturer, writer.

Raven - Magic: Supernatural abilities. The carrier of prayers. The ability to work with the four elements and smoke.

Mountain Lion - Leadership: Great responsibility. To lead many people by example.

Lynx - Secrets: The keeper of ancient knowledge, lost or hidden information. Memories of spiritual past lives.

Buffalo - Prayer and Abundance: The gift of powerful prayers, used to help others. A direct connection to the spirit world.

Mouse - Scrutiny: The gift of organization. Seeing the obvious and fine detail.

Owl - Deception and Death: Omen of impending danger. The loss of someone - death. Great wisdom and knowledge. Represents the darkness and night time.

Beaver - Builder: Your personal foundation. Your Family. A hard worker.

Opossum - Diversion: Using strategy. Playing dead to make your enemies think they've won. Then to regroup and move forward.

Crow - God's Laws: This magical bird represents the supernatural. The freedom to move between Heaven and Earth. The ability to see into the past and the future. The Universal Laws.

Fox - Observation: Cunning strategy. The protector of family even in the face of danger. Camouflage.

Squirrel - Gathering: Preparing in advance for change. Clutter of the mind. Cleansing of old thoughts and the clearing of people and material belongings.

Dragon Fly - Change: Personal transformation. Illusion, things may not be what they appear to be. Take a second look at things.

Armadillo - Limitations: To protect oneself. Knowing boundaries. Learning not to be critical of self.

Badger - Healer: The gift of understanding natural herbs and holistic medicine. Aggressiveness.

Rabbit - Fear: Fear of the unknown. The ability to face your fears and walk through them.

Turkey - Saintly: The medicine of mystics and saints. Purity of heart and of intent. Personal sacrifice for the highest good of all.

Ant - Patience: Teaching the importance of working together as a team. Each person is significant in the big picture. We are all equal.

Weasel - Ingenuity: The stealth ability to move around

without being noticed. Clever intelligence.

Horse - Power: Physical strength. The ability to travel in the spirit world and on the astral planes. Healing qualities.

Lizard - Dreamer: The art of dreaming. The ability to dream someone into your dreams. The doorway into the spirit world. Astral travel. Spirit communication.

Frog - Detoxifying: The bringer of the rain. Cleansing and purification. The ability to transmute negative energy. The ability to work with water.

Swan - Seer: Grace. The late bloomer in life. The gift of sight later in life. Ability to work in the dream time.

Dolphin - Breath of Life: A messenger to humanity. A person who works with God's children. A great affinity with water. Dolphin brings information in dreams.

Whale - Record Keeper: The ability to access past life records. The carrier of information in ones soul, to help us remember. The gift of remembrance.

Bat - Rebirth: Represents our natural journey of death and rebirth. A shaman's death, releasing an old way of life that no longer serves. Nocturnal, active at night.

Spider - Creativity: Female energy. To create joy in ones life through art, writing, or inspired work. The creator of the alphabet.

Humming bird - Joy and Beauty: A fragile energy that represents joy, beauty, and love. The importance of balance and harmony in life. Symbol for art, music, and food.

CHAPTER

18

TIME AND ITS
REAL MEANING

*M*any people don't understand the true concept of time. Time is an earthbound concept that since the dawn of mankind has been a measure. Daybreak and sunset were the first concepts and measure of time. The cycles of the moon regulated time periods of one month. Later came recognition of the seasons, Winter, Spring, Summer and Fall. The repetition of these natural cycles allowed mankind to plan and regulate their lives.

Later, we started to measure time in smaller increments until each period of light and darkness became distinct and measured time periods. Still later, we split days into smaller segments of time and measured them in hours and minutes. As technology developed, our count of time became more accurate and seconds were added to the picture.

Now in the age of micro electronics and splitting of the atom, leaps in science allow us to measure nano seconds, a measure of thousandths of each second.

So we can split time into smaller and smaller pieces in our quest for accuracy and knowledge.

In the universe there is no measure of time. The universe and God are eternal, they've always been here, long before any life on Earth and will remain forever, long after our sun has died and Earth is a barren dead planet.

Spirits and Angels are not constrained by time, they move by thought alone, they can move wherever they want and whenever they wish. In the spirit world there is no past, present or future, there is only eternal existence. This is a confusing concept for us to understand.

When we pray or meditate and ask for a sign, it's pointless to look at a clock and wait for a response within our measure of time. You may have an immediate response, but it could be a sign that shows within hours, weeks or even months. We must understand that our concepts are different to those of the spirit world.

Earthbound spirits have no concept of time, and so we may see ghosts and manifestations clothed as Roman soldiers, ancient Greeks or as visitor from any period of history. The ghost of Anne Boleyn is frequently seen wandering around the Tower of London, but her spirit - like others - has no concept of time.

They do not realize that their earthly bodies have been dead for hundreds or thousands of years. Many of the ghosts that we see are seeking a way into the light and wander aimlessly, time is but a distant memory for them.

As our technology allows us to see more and more of the vastness of the universe it has become obvious that our count of time is not perfect. Time as we know it is changing; scientists are moving away from clocks and chronometers and realizing that time itself can be stretched and even stopped.

Today those processes are not fully understood, although we know that theoretically it is possible to move backward and forward through time. Time travel will be an accepted form of travel in the future.

Once science, spirituality and faith are blended together our scientific research will explode and magnificent discoveries will be made. Science will have reached its next stage of evolution.

CHAPTER

19

EARTH CHANGES

*P*hysical Changes Are Coming Soon.

Living in today's world is not a happy existence for many, many people. Over the years we've lost touch with our spiritual roots and the true values that once embraced all of mankind.

Spurning our evolution, racial histories and the hard lessons learned over past millennia, we're now too caught up in technology and greed to realize that we're throwing away our old and honored values in a never satisfied quest for more and more materialistic gains.

It's a race that we can't win. Every advance in technology and lifestyle that we gain pushes the balance of life further away from its equilibrium. We're all moving farther away from our links with the spiritual world.

Global corporations constantly rape the Earth in ever deeper searches for raw materials, converting them into consumer products that kill our own oceans and rivers with ever more toxic pollutants - choking the very life from the planet that sustains us.

We use up the Earth's resources, both material and energy sources at a faster and faster rate. Our rainforests are stripped of life to a point there will be nothing left. Mankind abuses the very planet we need to sustain the basics of life, nuclear explosions, underground testing, pollution and pillaging of resources all contribute to our mad dash for self-destruction. A recent study showed that if the oil companies manage to extract what little is left of the petroleum from our Earth during the next ten years we won't have enough air to breath. Right now we're all on a race to our own ruin.

In addition to the physical damage we're wreaking on our environment and planet, mankind has also lost contact with the spiritual world. Anger, hatred, fear, lust and greed have clouded our vision and has pushed us away from the spirit world. The turning away from spiritualism means that we have lost touch with the power of love and charity, we need to have empathy with all living things.

Mother Earth is really unhappy, she's been soaking up negativity for far too long and the time for change is now.

A change is necessary for Mother Nature to cleanse herself and go through a process of renewal, changes that are necessary in order for men of all races, colors and creeds to co-exist with each other, the planet, nature and the spirit world.

Many people are aware that something is drastically wrong with our lives. There is a great underlying sense of dissatisfaction with the way things are right now on our planet. More and more people are looking for a solution to our problems, and now is the time to start uniting as a group for a global cause.

*   *   *

It's important that all the people of the planet realize that we all share a living planet, Mother Earth is a live breathing entity within herself.

We are all a part of Mother Nature, as much as the plants, trees, rocks, seas, skies and all the other components that comprise nature. We are her children and Mother Nature feeds and clothes us. We should respect the Earth and Mother Nature, the Native American people have done this since the beginning of time. They are the caretakers of Mother Earth and the most knowledgeable of the Earth Changes and are connected to her spirit.

Psychics and other spiritual people in touch with the fabric of our world sense that changes are coming, and are needed, if mankind is to survive.

Massive changes are coming on a global scale, and they will come sooner rather than later. They will be cataclysmic in nature and will unfortunately lead to great death and suffering on a worldwide scale - those who survive will have their values changed forever.

It's possible to predict the coming changes.

I see a time within the next few years when there will be great upheavals. The physical geography of our planet will undergo radical changes.

Some of those changes have already started. Coastlines are moving inland, not at the normal rate of land erosion - but so very rapidly such as the West Coast of California and here in South Florida. Lower Miami, Homestead and the Florida Keys are being eroded at ever increasing rates.

Southern Florida will ultimately be taken back by the sea, as far North as Lake Okeechobee.

There are other notable and recorded changes that have just started. The Polar ice caps are shifting and so melting at increasing rates, the planet's magnetic fields are moving at a measurable rate. Holes in the ozone layer are becoming larger and exposing more of the Earth's surface to the sun's harmful ultraviolet rays.

Hurricanes, earthquakes, fires, floods, tornadoes, tidal waves - all the great historic natural catastrophic events will increase in force and frequency. Coastlines around the world will be devastated as the seas advance and force us to re-write our maps.

Once dormant volcanoes will again spew mounds of lava and massive clouds of volcanic ash will obscure the sky, hastening in death and pestilence for millions. Volcanoes that have been dormant for years will activate again. We are truly facing a Doomsday scenario.

Populated landmasses we know today will sink below the waves and other lost lands such as the Lost Paradise of Atlantis will rise again from the sea floor.

The ancient land of Lemuria will resurface off the west coast of South America and Easter Island will once again become a mountain top.

The changes will continue as climate patterns alter. We will suffer a complete weather reversal. Hot areas will become cold, and frozen lands will become hot. These changes will bring about upheavals as the man made socio-economic society crumbles into anarchy, wars and starvation. Deaths will be measured in the billions, as the world becomes a great charnel house.

This is the time of purification, cleansing, and re-birth. It is the time some religions call Armageddon or the end times. It is not the actual destruction of our planet. It is the end of the world, as we have known it to be. It is a new beginning, a better way of life living in peace and unity.

Socio-Econmic Changes

Today we live in a high tech society geared to an ever increasing dependency on electricity, fuel, televsion, communications and computers. Each of us in the western world, is little more than a cipher in a government mainframe computer. Our lives are recorded and measured from birth until the grave.

We are measured in terms of our wealth and potential spending power, as the nameless corporations that run our lives and the dictates of government corrupt the true values of life. Honesty and integrity have become meaningless chips, discarded from the roulette table of modern life.

The massive changes coming in the physical world will herald revolutions in each of the world's governments. Take a moment to consider what will happen when the plug is pulled.

Our dependency on technology will soon be revealed as our egotistical weaknesses.

We will see the collapse of global and domestic financial empires. Money will become valueless as money markets and foreign exchanges collapse.

Governments will become impotent as the physical changes swallow seaports and low lying cities. Their total collapse will be hastened by the failure of monetary systems. Money, the raw material of all democratic governments will be useless and taxation will disappear, unable to pay their way the governments will experience a complete breakdown in their power bases; armies will be emasculated as soldiers walk home to their loved ones.

Western medicine and pharmaceutical companies are going to change radically. They are being forced to integrate holistic medicines and alternative forms of healing into their obsolete health practices.

The collapse of individual governments will herald a close of armed aggression and there will be peace on Earth for the first time in thousands of years.

Individual nations will join forces to survive as governments collapse, unable to cope alone with the Earth changes. Nations and nationalism, the false pride that has spawned many acts of aggression and wars through the ages, will disappear as the world's survivors take rule into their own hands. Common man will again rule in one world government. Power taken not by the force of arms but by necessity. Mankind will need to pull together and join forces if the race is to survive.

Within a short space of time we will be thrown back into the Middle Ages as technology fails us. We will revert to bartering to sell our goods, as we need to trade produce between ourselves to survive. This will lead to an increase in honesty and clarity of mind unknown to many people today. We will all come to understand the true value of charity and there will be a great outpouring of love throughout mankind as at last we each start to care for our brothers and sisters.

Religion

Religions, based on man made dogma and credo, fear and segregation are already undergoing change today. Christian, Jewish, Moslem and all other religions will fall away, impotent and unable to deal with the impending Earth changes.

Many smaller or splinter faiths and religions will be exposed for what they truly are. Catholicism, Jehovah's Witnesses, Mormons and others will be seen as fear and money based credos. They will have no place in the coming world.

Already the silent majority of people know it is morally wrong to try and force change with the bomb and the bullet. Jews and Moslems attack each other with animal like ferocity while Roman Catholic and Protestant Christians kill men, women and babies with a blind indifference in Northern Ireland - each side claiming the killings are carried out in the name of God.

The lack of religious tolerance is one of the great hypocrisies of our time. Religions should teach love, peace and understanding, not intolerance and the suppression of others with differing views. Intolerance and segregation will prove to be the undoing of man made religions and when the Earth changes arrive, the failure of today's religious leaders to help the common man will result in people turning their backs on the religions we know today.

When religions have failed to help mankind, they will fall from favor. But mankind will realize that there is only one true God, and that God is the true love and light in our universe.

Then there will be a one God religion, a religion that is based on love, charity, compassion and understanding. Once we choose the right path and start to live our lives in accord with God's Universal Laws and the higher truths, then we shall be able to save ourselves.

Within this next decade, there will be a great shift and people will find themselves changing their existing viewpoints, beliefs, thoughts, values and intolerances. Everything will alter when we realize that if we don't change our ways as a race then we will destroy humanity and the Earth.

Avoiding the Catastrophe

Mother Nature is ready for a rebirthing process and that will inevitably cause problems for mankind, even though we are a part of the process. We are connected to her and the spirit world and actions, thoughts and events that we initiate have an effect throughout the heavens.

There is no doubt that major Earth changes are coming, and will bring with them horrific death and destruction that will affect every man, woman and child on the planet. Governments and nations will fall and religions will be powerless to protect or sustain mankind through its darkest hours.

Now is a very special time in the evolution of humanity. We are at the threshold of change, and we have an opportunity to step through the doorway and ascend to a higher consciousness.

As we take that journey, our energy vibration becomes higher and we then invite God and his angels into our lives. The Spirit World understands the great damage we are doing to ourselves and to the Earth. They will try to help us to raise our vibration and bring us closer to our full potential.

The end of the world as we know it is not destiny, and it is not an unchangeable fact; we can stop it from happening. With the intervention of the spirit world we can avert disaster. We can make good use of this special time and move to a higher state of being.

Enlightenment

To move over the threshold to a new consciousness, we have to understand on an individual basis, each of us must have a spiritual awakening.

Only by letting our spirit guides and angels into our lives can we co-exist in the future with Mother Nature. We must each raise our consciousness, for a new awareness is upon us, and use the tremendous power of prayer in order to move on to a better way of life, a life filled with oneness and love. The power in prayer will invite your spirit guides and Angels to come closer to guide and council you through out life. By doing this you create a new awareness and will better co-exist with Mother Nature. Raising your consciousness will move you into a better way of life, a life filled with a feeling of oneness with the universe and God's unconditional love. Each soul shifting their consciousness will make a difference, an improvement for humanity. As mankind joins in numbers, these improvements will grow into solutions for a perfect Earth.

It's time to merge our world with the spirit world. Only then will there be a vibrational shift in the elements and from that will flow enlightenment, as we acknowledge our true selves. It's our graduation time, and we must not fail ourselves individually or the future of mankind. Let me assure you, one person does make a difference.

The Age of Enlightenment is here and we must seize the opportunity with both hands and an open heart. We must recognize the New Awareness, put away our toys and tools of self gratification and reconnect to God. I wish mankind everywhere peace and the foresight to acknowledge this time for change.

And the seventh Angel sounded his trumpet
and there were great voices
in Heaven saying:
The kingdom of Heaven will
become one with the kingdom of Earth
and the Lord will reign forever and ever.

– Revelations 11:5

CHAPTER

20

THE UNIVERSAL LAWS

*U*niversal Laws are higher truths created by God as a guideline to give direction to humanity. All of the master teachers who have walked this earth have taught, and have lived their lives to demonstrate the reality of these laws.

The Power of Creation

The Universal Laws are God's unchangeable spiritual Laws. These laws give us the power to create our earthy life and to advance our soul's growth. These laws were imparted to be used as tools given to mankind as a gift, to be applied so he could create anything we would like to experience.

People have said to me, "We don't create our life...life just happens to us." Well I am here to tell you; we are in charge of our destiny, God has bestowed this gift to us.

How do we construct our life? Consciously or

unconsciously everyone follows these steps of creation. First we think it. Every situation, concept, or opportunity that comes to us started as a single thought. Positive and negative thoughts do manifest into reality. Thoughts are energy and energy never dies. Artwork, inventions, college degrees, medical cures, and even murder, all things start with a single thought. Look at the hypochondriac, there is nothing wrong with the physical body at first, but by constantly dwelling on illness they eventually manifest a sickness. The power of our mind can create miracles or disasters, which do you choose to create?

Monitoring our thoughts becomes important. Try it for a day. Listen to the constant chatter in your mind. What is your mind saying? "Gee I look fat today. I'm not smart enough. I don't feel good. I can't accomplish that." Fear and self hatred must be erased from our consciousness. They are our biggest enemies. The wasteful, negative chatter can go on twenty-four hours a day seven days a week if we allow it.

We must edit our thoughts and reprogram the mind. Learn to see the good in all things. Look for the positive attributes in people, situations, and in ourselves. Even in the negative, there is a positive lesson to be learned. Make an effort to put away judgement and come from a loving place in your heart. By transforming negative mind chatter into positive inspiration we can change our life path. Positive thinking is truly an art form.

The second step in creation is visualization. In your minds eye, see what you want. In order to create something, you must know what it is that you want. See the positive outcome.

The third step is to speak it. Words are powerful; talking about your aspiration will help to bring it into fruition. You are invoking life into your idea. Always speak positively.

The fourth step is to take action. Put forth the effort to make your dream a reality. Be persistent. Take the steps necessary to create the outcome you want in the physical plane.

The most important step you must do while you are thinking it, seeing it, and speaking about it, is to believe it. All things are possible with faith. If you think that something is impossible, then it is impossible for you. Your personal belief system creates your reality. Faith is the essence of things hoped for, with confidence in the unseen. Then give thanks to God and be grateful for the abundance she bestows on us.

You have the power of creation, these are truths you will find within God's Universal Laws.

The Universal Laws are:

The Law of Love - This is the Prime Universal Law from which the others flow. It is the prime law that governs the Universe. By giving your love to individuals, animals, and the Earth you have the ability to transmute all negative things to positive.

Love is God in manifestation and the strongest magnetic force in the universe. Do unto others as you have them do unto you. Unselfish love and good will towards others is the key to all things. Apply unconditional love to people and to situations and you will see dramatic change in the reactions of others and in your life.

The Law of Forgiveness - To forgive someone is to exercise love in the highest form. To forgive another is to heal ones self and set yourself free. To harbor hatred for someone or cling to emotional wounds is the root cause of bitterness and much disease. Forgiveness is divine and the highest teaching.

The Law of Reincarnation - Is the contract we made in the spirit realm: promising to learn lessons through the physical experiences. The planet Earth is only one place where we can choose to incarnate. Reincarnation is the soul's journey, lifetime after lifetime of polishing and refining our spirit to perfection.

The Law of Inner Guidance and Intuition - Listen to the small voice inside and the feelings that move us, we are always able to connect with direct inspiration. Intuition will point the way without explanation. Your intuition or higher-self, is connected to Universal Intelligence, God, which is all knowing.

Do not confuse ego with intuition. Man receives setbacks whenever he is too confident. The conscious mind or ego cannot be trusted; whereas, our higher self is part of God and is perfect. We must edit our thoughts, consciously erasing the negative. Intuition is always the way our Angels and Spirit Guides speak to us, remember it is the voice within.

The Law of Cause and Effect - Known as karma. You will receive back only that which you give. Positive and negative deeds, thoughts and words will return to you with the same force or intent as they were done or said. What you sow, so shall you reap.

If you love everyone, love will come back to you; if you criticize others, you will be criticized yourself. For every choice there is a consequence, for every action there is a reaction.

The Law of Prosperity - The measure of a person's self worth and self love. Man can only receive what he believes he is worthy of receiving and he must balance prosperity by giving and receiving in equal parts.

We never get more than we believe we are worthy.

The Law of Non-resistance - As long as we resist a situation it will stay with us. Walk through your fears, face the situation and it will no longer have power over you. Know God protects you. When we resist a person or a situation, we are in fact seeing two powers instead of one. As in: Good versus Bad.

Once you choose or decide that there is only one true power - the power of God, then non-resistance no longer applies. When you use non-resistance with wisdom you understand that life is a flow, a balance and in having faith that everything will work out because of your beliefs.

The Law of the Spoken Word - What you say about another person will be said about you and what you wish for someone you are wishing for yourself. Choose your words wisely. Use your words for three purposes, to heal, bless or to prosper.

Because of the vibratory power of words, whatever man voices he begins to attract. Our words have power and we invoke thoughts and intent through our words. Some people say affirmations to train themselves to be more positive and to help create a desired outcome.

Be careful what you ask for, because you will get it. People who continually speak of disease invariably attract it. If you wish someone bad luck, we will only attract bad luck to ourselves. If you aid someone to success you are aiding them, but also aiding yourself. The intent has to be pure, if not the results will be negative or null and void.

The Law of Faith - Fearlessly knowing the Divine manifests all desires and giving thanks for all things large or small, "According to your faith be it given unto you." Faith is believing in a greater power, our creator. There is something more than we see, feel, hear, or even know. Faith is also believing in ourselves because we are a part of God. Faith is unseen but even so it is always there.

The Law of Thought - The strengths of our thoughts and beliefs create our reality. Thoughts of goodwill with pure motive creates great protection for the person who sends it. Love your enemies and bless them with your thoughts. Feeding negativity with more negativity only escalates a battle. Loving thoughts will transmute the situation. Thought is energy, it never dies. It manifests unto the physical world, unto someone, something or someplace. Thought is our intent that is directed towards the world. Thoughts are energy, they never die.

The Law of Grace - The Law that transcends Karma. This enlightened state awaits those who have overcome all worldly beliefs and accept their divine right of perfection. Once you have attained a higher state of consciousness you are demonstrating by living, these truths, which places you in a state of grace.

*   *   *

My hope is that each reader frees him and herself from self-imposed limitations. Think positive: change your internal programming, make a firm decision to think positive loving thoughts. Visualize your dreams, goals, and aspirations then work toward making them a reality. The mind is the builder of your future.

You have no one to blame for the way your life has turned out. You have created what you have become by the choices and decisions that you have made along life's journey. By taking personal responsibility for ourselves we can change the outcome of our lives at any time.

The object of life is to learn to create the positive and erase the negative fear and doubt from the mind. Man's only enemy lies within himself.

God has given us these Universal Truths to help us, so that we may choose to create fulfilling and wondrous lives without limitation.

**For he will give His Angels charge
concerning you
to guard you in all your ways.**

– Psalms 91:11

TWENTY QUESTIONS

*I*n private most people want me to answer personal questions, but I have included the twenty most frequently asked questions by the public from TV, radio, and lectures.

1. Who is God?

God is the Creator, the Supreme Being, and the Universal Consciousness. She is everything and nothing; he is the all of the universe and contains all aspects of feminine and masculine energy. God created the universe, the heavens and mankind, he is a part of each one of us. God is love and the internal light. We are all God's children and we are an extension of God, created from unconditional love.

2. What are Angels?

Angels are God's helpers, the messengers of God created for specific tasks. They come from unconditional love and only know goodness. They appear to us in a familiar guise, they take on a characteristic appearance that is comfortable to us or sometimes as a brilliant light. They are a form of energy and only appear to us for specific reasons to assist humanity. Angels are the very essence of God and represent his great love for each of us.

3. What happens when we die?

Everyone has a soul and each soul has a free will and choice, even in death. The majority of soul's travel into the light with their helpers, although some souls choose not to travel into the light and remain earthbound. Some souls do not believe in eternal life and so are confused when they leave the human form. They may remain for some time in the astral planes, although ultimately every soul will return to the heavens with the assistance of their Guardian Angels and Spirit Guide.

4. What is Heaven?

Heaven is a very large space, a place that is a higher realm than the Earth plane and is where spirits, Angels, and God reside. In Heaven there is only unconditional love, all is magnificently beautiful and perfect. Heaven comprises seven levels and contains many different places within it. Paradise is but a part of Heaven, for Heaven includes places of learning and the Hall of the

Akashic Records. Heaven is a place as big as the universe, but in a different space and place to our world. To truly describe Heaven with words is impossible. Our language lacks depth and fails to express the beauty and the emotions of a place of ultimate perfection.

5. Do we 'come back' to Earth?

Yes, our souls or spirits reincarnate, but only up to the time until when our spirit has gained sufficient knowledge, wisdom and love that it can move to another, higher level in the spirit world. Then the spirit evolves to a new level of consciousness and no longer needs to reincarnate on Earth.

6. Is my destiny fixed?

Certain experiences and lessons are fixed, they are in our soul's blueprint. We have opted to incarnate for specific reasons and some events are contracted for this incarnation. A person's free will and choice has an effect and can alter the life path that had been pre-planned for the soul's growth.

7. How do I create my future?

Everybody can create their own future by living and being in the moment, in other words live in the present, be conscientious, understand what you are thinking, doing and saying - be positive and know what you want, visualize it, and have faith - for that is what will create your future. We each have our own free will and choice, which enables us to choose any path. We can choose the best path by using our higher consciousness to guide us.

10. How can I relay messages to my deceased loved ones?

We all have the ability to pass our thoughts and words to our departed loved ones. Prayer and meditation open the portal that allows us to communicate directly with spirits. They hear every thing we say.

11. Is there gender in the spirit world?

Spirits are energy, they have no specific gender, but they appear in a manner that we are more comfortable with in this world. Spirit guides often choose a sex, usually from their last incarnation. In the spirit world there is no need for a sexual identity, unless a soul chooses one versus the other.

12. Is homosexuality a sin against God?

No, God is a God of love, he is not judgmental and loves us all equally. God gave us free will and our sexual preference is just another one of those choices.

I believe the reason that some souls choose to be homosexual is because they recall many past lives in which they were of the same gender. When they incarnate in this life, although they physically have a different gender the soul still recalls and prefers their previous lives as a member of the opposite sex.

13. Is Abortion a Sin?

No, before being born a human embryo is a biological growth that has not been joined with a soul. A psychic can clearly see a soul around the pregnant mother, awaiting the birthing process before joining with the biological body.

Towards the end of the term or at birth, the soul is joined with the baby. So if the fetus is aborted, it is not attached to a soul and is not a child of God.

To abort or not is an action, a choice, that can be made by women during pregnancy and a choice that demonstrates a woman's free will. It is an essential part of the human psyche and not a matter of religious opinion.

14. Does God have a favorite Religion?

No, God is universal, without gender, he/she is all things to all men. God is love and light itself and does not need man-made rules and limitations. Language and religion are man-made systems of communication and control, devices designed by man to keep society running under strict controls. Throughout the ages, leaders, both political and religious have imposed their own values on society, claiming to be speaking for God: this is untrue, God communicates with us in many varied ways, but not through the dogma of a structured fear based religion.

All souls enter Heaven irrespective of their religion on Earth. God does not play favorites or prefer one religion or sect. Jews, Gentiles, Moslems, Buddhists and all other religious followers are treated equally in Heaven, and earthbound religions are left behind as a spirit moves into the continuing cycle of life.

More important than any man made religion is a person's purity of soul, that is our guarantee of a place in Heaven.

15. Who is the Devil?

The concept of the Devil is a fiction created by man to control man. Religion controls mankind through fear. Most religions preach that a good person goes to Heaven while a bad person goes to Hell, this is incorrect, there is no place called Hell and there is no Devil, as taught by religion.

16. Is reincarnation a truth or a myth?

Reincarnation is a truth: it is a part of the soul's

evolution. We all re-visit this world in other human forms to continue our spirit's experiences and learning. We chose to experience different genders, race, religion, economic and social status. Without reincarnation it would be impossible for the soul to progress to the next stage. The objective of reincarnation is to polish and perfect the soul especially while here on earth in human form.

Some societies perpetuate the myth of humans reincarnating as animal or insects. This however is untrue. Humans do not return to Earth as part of the animal kingdom. Animals are another type of God's children and have their own spiritual evolution.

17. Why does God allow starvation, war, and disease?

God has given us all solutions and resources for ending all of our problems. He has also given us free will. Abominations to mankind are of man's doing, we have chosen these things, NOT God.

We have the knowledge to stop world hunger, we have the solution to end pollution from fossil fuels and the raping of Mother Earth of her natural resources. Sources of free energy were discovered many years ago.

We can cure many major diseases; but many of the new technical solutions are purposely kept away from the public, because the medical industry makes tremendous profit by continuing to use older outdated and ineffective procedures. Everyone in the medical industry food chain benefits from stifling medical advances and keeping the world's population in a state of ignorance of the newer advances in medicine.

We must stop killing each other in the name of religion and God. We must stop making excuses for ourselves and not judge others.

17. What is Déjà vu?

Déjà vu translated means "seen again." It is an experience we sometimes have when we feel we have visited a place, or seen a person before, but we can't remember that previous event.

Déjà vu can onset very suddenly and we are surprised that we seem to intuitively know a great deal about a place or person, right down to the smallest detail. These apparent tricks of memory are really a soul's memory recall of a familiar place or person from a past life. Déjà vu is a 'now happening' demonstration of a past life event.

Or it can be a current event that evokes a memory of an event that happened before. A memory that has taken place in the spiritual plane that is now taking place in the physical realm.

18. Do All Angels have wings?

No, some Angels do not have wings. They adopt a more human like form. All of the Archangels have huge sets of wings, wings that are very large and beautiful. Some of the Earth Angels have wings too, but they are smaller.

Fairies have translucent butterfly like wings.

19. Where do you get your information?

I often use the analogy of a radio. It's as if I put my antennae out into the universe and tune into the highest frequency. I connect to the universal consciousness where all information is stored. It is a conscious state of meditation, being connected to your God-Part-Self and letting the information flow.

20. What happens in a 'Spiritual Reading' with you?

When people call to make an appointment only the first name is given and a phone number to confirm the session. No other personal information is wanted. The day of, I always start a private session with a prayer for my client and I give thanks for the personal information I am about to receive while opening myself up to hearing the messages from the spirit world. I ask the client to say a silent prayer welcoming their Guardian Angels and Spirit Guides to come forward if they have a message.

After the prayers are said, each reading is different. No two people ever have the same issues. Each person's counseling is unique, I am directed to give very specific personal information. People come for many reasons, some don't even know why they've come until after the reading. I am blessed to be able to help people, but I know I am only the messenger.

Make yourself familiar with Angels,
and behold them frequently in spirit,
for without being seen,
they are present with you.

– Saint Francis De Sales

CHAPTER

22

SPIRITUAL TERMS

Akashic Records

Sometimes called the book of life. A record kept by each soul that includes words spoken, deeds and thoughts. This is an eternal record of every experience and life the soul encounters.

Archangels

Angels of the highest order, they are the Angels closest to God.

Aura

The colorful electro-magnetic field that radiates from and around a physical body. Sometimes referred to as the 'over-soul', it is the part of the soul that can be seen with the eye.

Blue Ray Children

Highly evolved spiritual children that represent the next evolutionary stage of mankind. Sometimes called Indigo Children.

Chakra

The human body has seven energy centers called Chakras. A psychic can see these colorful energy centers in a person's aura or spiritual body. The spiritual energy centers are directly linked to the physical health of the human body. When in perfect working order they are seen as bright, vibrant vortexes of energy.

Channel

A person who has the ability to access the universal consciousness and translate information from the cosmos or from spirits.

Clairaudiance

The ability to hear sounds from the Spirit realm

Clairvoyance

The ability to clearly see spirits or symbols and relay the information.

Déjà vu

A soul memory recall of a familiar place or person from a past life. A past life event memory.

A current event that evokes a memory of the event

happening before. A memory that has taken place in the spiritual plane that is now taking place in the physical realm.

Ego

Our conscious mind that passes judgement and makes decisions based on appearances or intelligence.

Guardian Angels

Two specific Angels are assigned to each of us. They never leave us from our birth, they help and protect us during our life and continue with us through the transformation we call death and into the afterlife.

God

The Supreme Being, the source of everything, the Universal Consciousness, the one creator of all that is.

God-part-self

Our higher consciousness, the part of the soul that is connected to God and that is perfect.

Karma

The Universal Law of cause and effect. What you sow, so you shall reap. Every action causes a reaction.

Kundalini Energy

Is the sexual and spiritual energy that is associated with the source of our life energy. Kundalini energy is stored in our root chakra or the energy center at the base of the spine. Kundalini energy is sometimes referred to as the fire within.

Medium

A person who has the ability to communicate with the otherside: departed loved ones, Angels, and spirit guides and other souls residing in the spirit world.

Near Death Experience

When the physical body experiences death and the soul leaves the body, travels to the spirit realm and then returns to the body with the remembrance of the experience.

Psychic

A person who has the ability to 'read' another persons energy or vibrations and relay accurate information about their past, present and future.

Psychic Empathy

The ability to feel the emotions and physical sensations of another, either a spirit or of a human.

Psychometry

The ability to 'read' objects or photos by tuning into the vibration or energy field surrounding that object and receiving information about it.

Reincarnation

The rebirth of a soul into a new body.

Silver Cord

The etheric cord that attaches the physical body to the spiritual body, the soul.

Soul

The spirit, the essence, or core of our being that is eternal.

Spirit Guide

A spirit that helps us with a specific aspect of our spiritual development while on Earth. We each have one Spirit Guide that stays with us from birth through death. Other sprit guides are assigned to us for different periods of time to help us through different phases of life.

Spiritual Reading

A personal counseling session with a Psychic Medium whom chooses to receive information only from God and his helpers.

Subconscious

A part of the mind that holds all memories. The subconscious mind acts as a filter for the conscious mind.

Telepathy

The ability to send and receive thoughts as a way of communicating with others.

The Council

A highly evolved group of twelve Ascended Masters, sometimes referred to as 'The Elders'. They are in charge of humanity's Karma. The Council is in charge of 'The Book of Life'.

Universal Intelligence

The mind of God. Sometimes called universal conscience.

Victim Soul

A person who has chosen to soak up a large amount of Karma for humanity.

The name Angel refers to their office,
not their nature.
You ask the name of its nature,
it is Spirit;
you ask its office,
it is that of an Angel,
which is a messenger.

– Saint Augustine

CHAPTER

23

TESTIMONIALS
& APPRECIATION

*M*y job as a messenger is not the easiest profession. It is a huge responsibility when someone comes to you for guidance, seeking answers to personal issues. I take my job very seriously. With Gods help, I counsel those in need.

The answers I relay from God, her Angels and Spirit Guides are often direct solutions to the client's problem and unfortunately, most people would prefer an easier route. You must realize it is hard for most people to look objectively at themselves, to really see their weaknesses and the problems that stem from them. It is much easier to point a finger at a parent, a spouse, or their environment than take personal responsibility for their life. My job as a messenger is to relay the information from 'Spirit' without editing. For those in denial, the directness of the message can be hard to swallow.

So when I receive confirmation that a client took heed of their reading, I receive personal satisfaction.

Enclosed you will find notes clients have written, a few gems that always brighten my day. A little appreciation and the ability to make a difference in someone's life are my motivators.

I give thanks to 'The Great Spirit' for allowing me to serve him and make a difference.

Michelle White Dove
PO Box 550966
Fort Lauderdale FL 33355

Jan. 28, 2000

Dearest Michelle,

You have had a great impact on my life!
Born and raised in a socialist country my spiritual knowledge was close to zero
although I have always been curious about supernatural events. In my twenties
and living in the U.S. I decided to search for "the truth". I investigated yoga,
meditation, New Age readings, spiritual seminars and finally I studied with a
Yogi for years. Always searching for answers trying to put all the puzzle pieces
together.

Ten years later I met you at one of your speaking events. I just want to tell you
how much my life changed after that. Attending your seminars and then taking
your class at NOVA, I learned the spiritual truths that transformed my life.
Mysteries of a Lifetime answered. Everything you taught made sense. You
have the ability to teach at a level everyone can understand.

Not only your spiritual teachings have had great impact in my life but also your
psychic abilities may have saved my life.   At one of your events you gave me a
warning that I had a growth in my female organs that needed to be removed. In
November of 1999, you warned me again, this time urgently telling me that I
needed to make an appointment with a specialist very soon, and that I must
take this warning seriously.

I took your advice and saw a specialist, and was scheduled for surgery
December 17, 1999. During surgery the doctor was so shocked by the size of
the huge tumor, he took a photograph of it. It was the size of a baby! If a tumor
of that size had ruptured, the poisons would have entered by bloodstream and
killed me.

I have recovered well and because of you, I feel great.

On another note, when you were giving me information about my health you
also told me to get prepared that I would loose my father soon. Jan 24th I
received word from Europe my father passed away. Your teachings about death
and the continuance of life on the other side have given me great comfort and
have eased my grief.

Dear Michelle, I can't thank you enough for everything you've done for me. I
am extremely impressed with your psychic abilities and your spiritual
knowledge. You have the ability to help humanity tremendously.

With Love and Respect,
Elaine

TESTIMONIAL

My name is Bobbie. I've has numerous health problems since I was in my early forties. Lately, however, I was overreacting to everything and sobbing constantly; I was hyper-reactive beyond the usual. I had heard about Michelle Whitedove from an acupuncturist that highly recommend her, so I thought it was worth a try to go to someone who could possibly 'see' my problem.

On March 3rd, during the course of my reading she told me that there was something wrong physically, "your hormones are all out of whack". She listed symptoms I had been experiencing, depression and weight gain. Then she grabbed her head, "Tumor" she said, then, "no, more like an aneurysm on the brain. It will rupture if you don't take care of it." She had already said so many accurate things, I was scared enough to lie my way into an MRI. My husband is a doctor, so as a scientist not very easily won over by psychics but when he heard the tape recorded reading, he was convinced I should proceed with medical tests.

We soon found Michelle was right; I have a benign tumor on my pituitary gland that was undetectable a year and a half ago. I went on medication immediately. If not treated, these tumors affect the optical nerve and can lead to blindness. Many of the exaggerated psychological symptoms have begun to disappear as treatment continues. Already my breasts are smaller and my reactivity is less. This Tumor explains a lot of mysteries in my body.

People have asked me "How did you find out about this Tumor?" I tell them if it wasn't for Michelle's insistence that I take her council seriously, I would have never known there was something 'wrong' with my brain. Her intuition was right. She is gifted!

Bobbie B.
Miami, FL

Michelle,
I Just wanted to say thank you again for all your help! To update you my six year old son John has really benefited from the time he spent with you. He has reiterated to me on three occasions that "She sure knows how to explain things that are complicated and makes them easy huh, mom?" He is a changed person.
Thanks Again, Linda

Michelle,

You gave me a reading in Feburary. I don't know why I was sent to you soon after my husband passed away, but I do know that now I can sleep at night and really look forward to it. I still feel the pain of him not physically here, but there is great joy in knowing that he will always be with me in spirit.

I think after seeing you I have helped several family members that were having a hard time dealing with his death.

Thank you for the peace in my heart.
Beth

Dear Michelle,
I was at your lecture tonight and truly enjoyed listening to you. You are an Angel! Thank you for spreading your beautiful words of love to us all. It was truly an honor to be in your presence and I thank God for the opportunity. You give so much of your divine self to the world, and I pray you know how much you are appreciated. You will be in my prayers, and I know the Angels will be assisting you.
With Love, Janet

Dear Michelle,
Thank you for your guidance. I just want to let you
know my mom passed away last Wednesday. I feel I
was better able to cope because of my reading with you.
I was originally surprised when you told me months ago
that her time was short, but I was able to come to terms
with her death in advance.   I had the opportunity to say
what had been left unsaid for a long time.
Thank you for everything, Carmen

Dear Michelle,
Just a note of thanks for the information you
were able to give to the police following the
murder of my husband. Your ability to see the
event 'as it happened' was amazing. The details
you gave, names of people and the circumstances
surrounding his death will certainly give the
police leads to work on. Now I am praying they
find the evidence to convict the suspects.
I truly appreciate your efforts, Regina

*For every soul,
there is a Guardian watching it.*

– The Koran

A Prayer

Lord, make me an instrument of Thy peace.
Where there is hatred, let me sow love;
Where there is injury, pardon;
Where there is doubt, faith;
Where there is despair, hope;
Where there is darkness, light;
Where there is sadness, joy.

Divine Master,
Grant that I may not so much seek
To be consoled as to console;
To be understood as to understand;
To be loved as to love;
For it is in giving that we receive;
It is in pardoning that we are pardoned;
It is in dying that we are born
Unto eternal life.

Michelle Whitedove is a renowned psychic medium and channel. She teaches spiritual development courses, conducts private counseling sessions and public lectures. Currently the host of her own 'Spiritual TV Talk Show' she uses her gifts to relay conversations from the spirit world to those in the physical world. Michelle has been featured on PBS television and has done numerous radio interviews in America as well as Europe.

For more information and a list of public appearances: www.michellewhitedove.com